ENTERTAINING THE SLIM WAY

Addison-Wesley Publishing Company
Reading, Massachusetts • Menlo Park, California
London • Amsterdam • Don Mills, Ontario • Sydney

ENTERTAINING THE SLIM WAY

Lou Seibert Pappas

Also by Lou Seibert Pappas:
Crossroads of Cooking
Greek Cooking
Party Menus
Bread Baking
Crockery Pot Cookbook
Salads/Casseroles Cookbook
Egg Cookery
Gourmet Cooking the Slim Way

Illustrations by Robert Rose

Library of Congress Cataloging in Publication Data

Pappas, Lou Seibert.
  Entertaining the slim way.

  Includes index.
  1. Entertaining. 2. Low-calorie diet--Recipes.
I. Title.
TX731.P292   642'.4   78-20890
ISBN 0-201-05667-4
ISBN 0-201-05666-6 pbk.

Copyright © 1979 by Addison-Wesley Publishing Company, Inc. Philippines copyright 1979
by Addison-Wesley Publishing Company, Inc.
ISBN 0-201-05666-6
ISBN 0-201-05667-4
ABCDEFGHIJ-MA-79

With love to Mary Tift,
an artist supreme,
whose joy and warmth
are an inspiration to me.

Introduction

The spotlight on healthy living is shaping today's lifestyle. A new cuisine is evolving: lighter, leaner, and delectably fresh. The emphasis is on an abundance of fruits, vegetables, fish, and poultry, swiftly prepared and artistically presented. In tandem with this approach there is a spiraling interest in physical fitness—in exercising and getting back to nature. The result of the overall effort is a wonderful feeling of buoyancy and sagacity, coupled with a ready-for-anything attitude. The total impact is a sharpening of all the senses.

It is only logical to share this new philosophy when entertaining. Guests appreciate fewer calories and less cholesterol while simultaneously savoring a captivating feast. The ethnic world of recipes is the ragtime of our table. Providing a lively, syncopated beat, new flavors and dishes spark our dining with delightful new experiences. For all occasions, in a kaleidoscope of patterns, here are menus for *Entertaining the Slim Way*.

Contemplate a Mexican weekend brunch for house guests, a sit-down Tuscany garden luncheon, a French wine-country picnic, an ultraeasy Greek "bandit style" dinner, a make-ahead Moroccan spread for 8, an Egyptian barbecue, a Scandinavian soup supper, or a Mandarin after-theatre repast. Plans for 60 different dining pleasures follow. These worldly menus are keyed to charm both family and guests with today's life-style cooking.

Portola Valley, California L.S.P.
January 1979

Contents

Entertaining with an International Ambience

Entertaining at home is staging a comeback. The joys of sharing with guests some of life's simpler pleasures in a sophisticated, sometimes ethnic style have been rediscovered. Table decor adds to this festive ambience, and small, unexpected touches often invoke the greatest praise. When you prepare the international menus in *Entertaining the Slim Way*, consider keynoting your table decor with some of these simple ideas:

*

Arrange eggplants, lemons, and artichokes in a copper bowl for a Mediterranean supper.

*

Center a table with a basket of sprouting, green Danish watercress, to be snipped at need.

*

Using napkins in bright colors, such as hot pink, orange, and purple, fold them in a fan shape and tuck them into wide-bowled wine glasses, alternating the colors around the table.

Fill Mexican hammered-tin birds with bunches of green grapes, yellow pom-pom mums, and ivy.

*

Use shells as a centerpiece, piling them into a crystal compote, and place a small one at each plate.

*

Float short, chunky candles and camelia or gardenia blossoms in a shallow tray of water.

*

Center a table with a basket or bowl of lemons, limes, oranges or kumquats, and daisies.

*

Let a bright, Chinese chicken-shaped basket cuddle fresh brioche at an early breakfast.

*

Pack onions with red, white, and yellow skins or new and old potatoes in a handled wicker basket with yellow daisies peeking out.

For a seafood dinner, tuck sheaths of dried seaweed and tiny cattails into a bowl of blue iris. Arrange on a sky blue cloth with deeper blue crown-folded napkins.

*

Focus on a thriving plant—a crock of yellow crocus bursting into bloom or a basket of strawberries turning from blossom to berry.

*

Let a vegetable basket, arranged like a bridal nosegay, serve as both centerpiece and crudité tray.

Part of entertaining with flair is to serve small courses in stages. Using a variety of patterns, textures, and complementary accents provides its own kind of fascination. Consider using plates of Danish rosewood, Egyptian hammered copper, or American pewter. Mix moderately-priced Oriental soup bowls among fine Imari ware. Introduce humble French butter pots, shiny individual copper ramekins, German wooden bread-and-butter boards, Portuguese meat terrines with animal-shaped lids, and Turkish copper serving pieces. Celebrate with both fine Limoges and simple stoneware. With such fresh and natural surprises adorning the table, the stage is set for entertaining with an international ambience.

Weekend Breakfasts

Mexican Brunch · Italian Breakfast ·
Intimate French Brunch · Alpine Breakfast ·
Bavarian Brunch · Sunday Petit-Déjeuner

Mexican Brunch Serves 6

Fruit Platter
Chile Jack Oven Omelet
Toasted Cinnamon Slices
Spiced Coffee

The Latin way of presenting a bounteous array of seasonal fruits on a breakfast tray makes a festive beginning for a brunch. Tuck a few blossoms—cyclamen, fuschias, camelias, nasturtiums—among the fruit for even more color. The oven omelet can be assembled a day in advance to be ready for last-minute baking. For a party mood, offer Sangria (see page 188). This menu has about 335 calories per person.

Fruit Platter

Arrange 6 to 8 spears of fresh pineapple, 6 to 8 watermelon wedges, several bunches of grapes, and some slices of peeled papaya on a platter. Garnish with lime wedges and flower blossoms. Makes 6 servings, about 75 calories each.

Chile Jack Oven Omelet

6 eggs
¾ cup water
¼ cup nonfat dry milk
½ teaspoon salt
½ teaspoon Mexican seasoning, or
⅛ teaspoon each oregano, garlic, cumin, and black pepper
1⅔ cups grated Monterey jack cheese
3 tablespoons chopped green chile peppers*

* To avoid using peppers that are too hot, buy canned whole chile peppers, slit them open, and remove the seeds and veins before chopping. (Canned diced chile peppers often include the too-hot seeds.)

Beat eggs until light and stir in water, powdered milk, salt, Mexican seasoning, cheese, and peppers. Pour into a lightly buttered 9-inch pie pan. ☆ Bake in a 350° oven for 35 minutes, or until puffed and golden brown. Cut into wedges. Makes 6 servings, and each contains about 200 calories.

☆ Prepare in advance to this point. Refrigerate, covered, up to 1 day. Increase the baking time by 10 minutes if chilled.

Toasted Cinnamon Slices

Slice a long loaf of French bread into 12 slices, spread them lightly with whipped, sweet butter, and sprinkle with a mixture of 1½ teaspoons cinnamon and 3 tablespoons sugar. Broil until toasted. Makes 6 servings, about 50 calories each.

Spiced Coffee

For each mug- or cupful of coffee, drop in 2 whole cloves, 1 cinnamon stick, and ½ teaspoon brown or raw sugar. Let steep before sipping. Each cupful has about 8 calories.

Italian Breakfast *Serves 8*

Winter Pears with Prosciutto
Verona Loaf
Breakfast Cheese
Espresso

A feathery, lemon-scented egg bread, juicy pears sliced and draped with smoked ham, a low-calorie breakfast cheese or natural cream cheese, and robust espresso make a splendid easy-to-serve repast in the Italian manner. Allowing for 2 slices of bread, 1 ounce of cheese, and 1 small pat of sweet butter, the calorie count is about 300 calories per person.

Winter Pears with Prosciutto

Just before serving, peel and slice 4 Comice or Anjou pears. Arrange 3 to 4 slices on each plate and cover each slice with 2 pieces of prosciutto. As an alternative, substitute melon wedges for the pears. Makes 8 servings, about 50 calories each.

Verona Loaf

1 package active dry yeast	1½ teaspoons vanilla extract
¼ cup lukewarm water	1 teaspoon salt
½ cup butter	3 eggs
2 tablespoons sugar	½ cup hot water
1 teaspoon freshly grated lemon peel	3¼ cups all-purpose flour
	1 egg white, lightly beaten

Sprinkle yeast into lukewarm water and let stand until dissolved, about 5 minutes. Beat 3 tablespoons of the butter with the sugar, lemon peel, vanilla, salt, and eggs. Pour in the hot water, beating until smooth, and stir in the yeast mixture. Gradually add flour, stirring in enough to make a soft dough. Turn onto a floured board and knead lightly. Place in an oiled bowl, cover with a damp towel, and let rise in a warm place until doubled in size, about 1½ hours. Punch dough down and return to the board. Knead lightly and roll into a rectangle about ½ inch thick. Cut the remaining 5 tablespoons butter into thin slices. Place half the slices in the center one-third of the rectangle. Fold an outer section of the dough over the center and place the remaining butter slices on top. Fold the remaining dough section to cover all. Roll out, making a strip 18 inches long. Fold this into 3 sections, wrap loosely in waxed paper, and refrigerate 20 minutes. Repeat twice, without adding more butter. On a floured board divide dough into 3 parts. Stretch the top of each piece by pulling it underneath to form a ball. Place in greased 9-inch baking pans. Cover and let rise in a warm place until doubled in bulk, about 3 to 4 hours. Brush with the egg white. Bake in a 350° oven for 30 to 35 minutes, or until loaves are golden brown and sound hollow when thumped. Remove from pans and let cool slightly. ☆ Serve warm, sliced, with sweet butter. Each loaf makes 8 servings, about 100 calories each.

☆ Prepare in advance to this point. After cooling for 15 minutes, slip the loaves into a plastic bag, seal tightly, and freeze. To reheat, thaw, wrap in foil, and bake in a 350° oven for 15 to 20 minutes.

Intimate French Brunch Serves 4

Asparagus Omelet
Sautéed Mushrooms with Herbs
Marinated Fruit Medley

This menu offers a versatile plan for many occasions—a spring brunch, a luncheon, or a light after-theatre supper. It is especially appealing in warm weather. Here, as always, choice fresh produce is essential. For a companionable aperitif, offer a Royal, a blend of champagne and raspberry liqueur or juice (see page 186). The approximate calorie count is 375 per person.

Asparagus Omelet

1 **pound fresh asparagus**
8 **eggs**
2 **teaspoons butter**
  Salt
  Freshly ground pepper
2 **tablespoons freshly grated**
    Parmesan cheese

Snap ends from asparagus and peel tough stalks. Slice on the diagonal into ½-inch pieces. Cook in boiling salted water for 3 to 4 minutes, or until crisp tender; drain. Heat an omelet pan over medium-high heat and add ½ teaspoon of the butter. Beat 2 eggs just until blended and season with salt and pepper to taste. Pour eggs in all at once and let set, lifting from the bottom to allow liquid portion to run underneath. Spoon one-fourth of the asparagus in a ribbon down the center, sprinkle with one-fourth of the cheese, and roll the omelet, turning it onto a warm plate. Repeat, making 3 more omelets. Makes 4 servings, 190 calories each.

Sautéed Mushrooms with Herbs

1 pound mushrooms
2 tablespoons butter
1 tablespoon lemon juice
¼ teaspoon salt
   Freshly ground pepper

2 tablespoons minced fresh
   parsley, chives, and tarragon,
   mixed together
2 tablespoons plain yogurt
2 tablespoons sour cream

Slice any large mushrooms; leave small ones whole. Melt butter in a large frying pan. When it sizzles, add mushrooms and lemon juice and sauté about 1 minute. Season with salt, pepper to taste, and herbs and spoon onto individual plates. Mix together the yogurt and sour cream, and garnish each serving of mushrooms with a spoonful of this mixture. Makes 4 servings, about 95 calories each.

Marinated Fruit Medley

1 mango
2 nectarines or peaches
½ small pineapple
1 cup strawberries
2 tablespoons orange
   liqueur (such as Cointreau
   or Grand Marnier)

Peel and slice the mango and nectarines. Peel and dice pineapple, discarding the core. Hull the strawberries. Place the fruit in a serving bowl and spoon liqueur over all. Let chill 1 hour. Makes 4 servings, about 90 calories each.

$\mathcal{A}$lpine $\mathcal{B}$reakfast _Serves 6_

Swiss Cinnamon Braid
Cheese Board
Eggs in the Shell
Crenshaw Melon
Coffee

This is a wonderfully easy weekend breakfast to set out for house guests.
The spicy, aromatic bread can be baked well in advance and frozen; let
thaw and reheat in foil to serve. The other elements go together readily at
the last minute. This menu has about 410 calories per person.

Swiss Cinnamon Braid

1   package active dry yeast
¼   cup lukewarm water
¼   cup butter
5   tablespoons sugar
1   teaspoon salt
2   eggs
½   cup hot water
3   cups unsifted all-purpose flour
1½   teaspoons cinnamon

Sprinkle yeast into warm water and let stand until dissolved, about 5
minutes. Place the butter, 2 tablespoons of the sugar, the salt, eggs, and
hot water in a mixing bowl and beat until blended. Add the yeast mixture
and beat smooth. Gradually add flour, beating smooth and adding just
enough to make a soft dough. Turn onto a lightly floured board and knead
lightly. Place in a bowl, cover with a towel, and let rise in a warm place
until doubled, about 1½ hours.

Punch dough down and return to board. Knead lightly and cut into 3 equal
pieces. Roll each into a strip about 18 inches long. Combine the remaining
3 tablespoons sugar with the cinnamon and sprinkle evenly over a 20-inch
piece of waxed paper. Roll the dough strips in this mixture, coating completely. Braid the strips, pinching the ends together and tucking them
underneath. Place on a greased baking sheet, cover, and let rise until

doubled, about 1 hour. Bake in a 375° oven for 30 to 35 minutes, or until golden brown. ☆ Makes 1 very large braid yielding about 3 dozen slices (70 calories per slice).

☆ After baking, the loaf may be frozen while still warm.

Cheese Board

Set out a wedge of Gruyère or jarlsberg cheese and a chunk of Canadian Cheddar, allowing about 1½ ounces per person. Makes 6 servings, about 150 calories each.

Eggs in the Shell

Place a dozen eggs in cold water, bring to a boil, and let simmer for 4 minutes (this leaves the centers still runny). Cool them immediately in cold water. Makes 6 servings, about 160 calories each.

Crenshaw Melon

Cut 1 Crenshaw melon into wedges and scoop out the seeds. Using a grapefruit knife, separate the fruit from the shell and cut each wedge into ¾-inch slices. Serve in the shell on plates lined with orange or lemon leaves. Makes 6 servings, about 30 calories each.

Bavarian *Brunch* Serves 6

German Pancakes
Cranberry Orange Juice
Coffee

For a special Sunday brunch serve German-style berry-filled pancakes for the entrée. Accompany with pink grapefruit halves or fresh juice and coffee. This light breakfast contains about 225 calories per person.

German Pancakes

4   eggs
1   cup water
¼   cup cornstarch
¼   cup nonfat dry milk
6   teaspoons butter
3   cups strawberries,
        blackberries, raspberries, or
        blueberries*
1   teaspoon cinnamon
1   tablespoon sugar

Place the eggs, water, cornstarch, and powdered milk in a blender or food processor. Blend just until smooth. Heat an 8-inch crêpe pan and add ½ teaspoon of the butter. When it stops sizzling, pour in just enough batter to cover the pan, tilting to let batter run. Cook over moderate heat until golden brown underneath and set on top. Repeat process to make about 11 more pancakes, buttering pan each time. ☆ Spoon ½ cup berries down the center of each crêpe. Mix the sugar and cinnamon and sprinkle over the fruit; roll up. Keep warm in a low oven until all are cooked. Makes 6 servings, about 150 calories each.

☆ The pancakes may be made in advance, kept wrapped in the refrigerator or freezer, and reheated in a moderate oven.

* When berries are out of season, substitute an apple filling. Peel and thinly slice 3 Golden Delicious apples and cook in a frying pan with ¼ cup water, 1 tablespoon sugar, and 1½ teaspoons lemon juice until apples are tender and liquid is evaporated, about 8 to 10 minutes. Spoon inside pancakes and sprinkle with ¼ teaspoon cinnamon.

Cranberry Orange Juice

1   cup cranberry juice, chilled
2   cups orange juice, chilled

Combine the juices and pour into juice or wine glasses. Garnish with a twist of lemon, if desired. Makes 6 servings, about 75 calories each.

Sunday Petit- Déjeuner

Serves 6

Omelets with Strawberries
Cylindrical Filbert Loaves
Orange Juice
Café au Lait or Filter Coffee

With a well-seasoned pan, individual omelets are one of the speediest and most savory ways to turn out eggs—even for half a dozen guests or more. Here they blend with traditional components of a French breakfast. One-pound coffee cans shape the cylindrical breads, making neatly sliced rounds. Other nuts, such as walnuts, pecans, or almonds, may substitute for filberts in the loaves. After baking, the whole nuts are sliced with ease. With café au lait and Mimosas (see page 187) this is a complete party meal. Allowing 2 slices of Filbert Loaf and a small pat of sweet butter, this weekend breakfast has about 350 calories per person.

Omelets with Strawberries

6	eggs
	Salt
	Freshly ground pepper
2	teaspoons butter
1	pint strawberries, hulled and sliced
2	tablespoons powdered sugar

Beat each egg individually, seasoning to taste with salt and pepper. Heat an omelet pan, add ½ teaspoon of the butter, and when it stops sizzling, pour in the egg. Cook until set, lifting to let liquid flow underneath. Place a spoonful of berries down the center of each omelet; roll up. Turn onto individual plates and spoon more berries on top. Dust lightly with powdered sugar. Makes 6 servings, about 110 calories each.

Cylindrical Filbert Loaves

1 package active dry yeast
¼ cup lukewarm water
¼ cup butter
2 tablespoons sugar
1 teaspoon salt
1 teaspoon vanilla extract
3 eggs
½ cup hot water
3¼ cups unsifted all-purpose flour
6 tablespoons filberts or slivered
    almonds

Sprinkle yeast into lukewarm water and let stand until dissolved, about 5 minutes. In a mixing bowl beat the butter, sugar, salt, vanilla, and eggs until blended. Mix in the hot water and dissolved yeast, beating smooth. Gradually add flour, stirring in enough to make a soft dough. Turn onto a floured board and knead lightly. Knead in the nuts. Place in a bowl, cover, and let rise in a warm place until doubled in size, about 1½ hours. Punch down and return to the board. Divide in 3 equal parts. Shape each part in a ball, and place the balls in greased 1-pound coffee cans. Cover and let rise until doubled, about 45 minutes. Bake in a 350° oven for 35 minutes, or until loaves sound hollow when thumped. Remove from oven and let cool 10 minutes; turn out of pans. ☆ Each loaf makes 6 servings, about 130 calories each.

☆ The loaves may be frozen, wrapped well, while still warm.

Sit-Down Luncheons

Provençal Lunch • French Salad Luncheon •
Pacific Salad Luncheon • Crab Season
Luncheon • A Tuscany Luncheon • A Burgundy
Party Luncheon • Harvest Luncheon • Parisian
Bistro Lunch

Provençal Lunch Serves 6

Ratatouille
Gruyère Soufflé
Baked Apples Rosé with Honey Snow

Elements of country dining in Provence mingle in this festive lunch or supper. Ideal for the harvest season, red peppers, tomatoes, eggplant, basil, and apples are essentials here. A sturdy and fascinating first course is ratatouille, an interplay of colorful vegetables that is excellent hot or cold. This one has the spark of crumbled white feta and bright green pistachios for an appealing topping. A light double cheese soufflé follows. Wine-steeped apples served with a fluffy honey sauce fill the dessert role. For a wine, consider a California Pinot Blanc, a French Muscadet, or a Vouvray. The calorie count for this refreshing lunch is about 450 per person.

Ratatouille

1 large eggplant, diced	¼ cup chopped fresh parsley
Salt	6 tablespoons chopped fresh basil
Freshly ground pepper	½ cup tomato sauce
2 large onions, finely chopped	3 ounces feta cheese, sliced or
2 teaspoons olive oil	crumbled
4 medium zucchini, chopped	2 tablespoons chopped pistachios

Sprinkle eggplant cubes with salt and let stand 15 minutes for juices to exude. Rinse under cold running water. Sauté onions in oil in a large Dutch oven or flame-proof casserole, cooking until glazed. Add zucchini and eggplant and cook 2 minutes. Season with the parsley, 4 tablespoons of the basil, the tomato sauce, and salt and pepper to taste. Cover and simmer for 30 to 40 minutes. ☆ To serve, spoon into a serving dish or platter and sprinkle with cheese, the remaining 2 teaspoons of basil, and pistachios. If desired, serve cold. Makes 6 servings, about 110 calories each.

☆ Prepare in advance to this point and keep refrigerated.

Gruyère Soufflé

6 eggs, separated
4 egg whites
⅓ cup plain yogurt
½ teaspoon salt
½ teaspoon dry mustard
1 cup grated Gruyère, jarlsberg,
  or Swiss cheese
½ cup grated Parmesan cheese

Beat all 10 egg whites until soft peaks form; set aside. Beat the 6 yolks until thick and lemon colored, then beat in yogurt, salt, and mustard. Stir in the cheeses. Add one-third of the whites to the yolks, mixing until blended; fold in remaining whites. Turn into a buttered 10½-inch round baking dish or a 1½-quart soufflé dish with a foil collar. ☆ Bake in a 375° oven for 25 minutes, or until puffed and golden brown. Makes 6 servings, about 190 calories each.

☆ Prepare in advance to this point. Let stand at room temperature up to 1 hour before baking.

Baked Apples Rosé with Honey Snow

6   large baking apples
½   cup orange juice
½   cup rosé wine, apple juice,
      or cider
½   cup honey
1   stick cinnamon
1   can (11 ounces) mandarin
      oranges
1   egg white
¼   teaspoon freshly ground
      nutmeg

Core apples and pare off 1 inch of the peel around the upper part of each. Arrange in a baking dish. In a saucepan combine orange juice, wine, ¼ cup of the honey, and the cinnamon stick, broken into pieces. Simmer until honey is dissolved and ingredients are blended. Pour this sauce over the apples. Bake in a 375° oven for 30 to 40 minutes, or until apples are barely tender. Drain oranges and spoon several sections inside each apple cavity. Baste with pan juices and bake 5 minutes longer. ☆ While the apples are baking, beat egg white until soft peaks form. Gradually add the remaining ¼ cup honey, beating until stiff. Blend in nutmeg. Serve with the warm apples. Makes 6 servings, about 150 calories each.

☆ The apples may be baked a day before serving and refrigerated. Reheat in a moderate oven.

French Salad Luncheon   Serves 4

Shrimp and Artichokes Richelieu
Hot Verona Loaf (see page 8)
Lemon Soufflé Custard

For a delightful luncheon entrée with a bit of a surprise, consider this intriguing salad. It is a specialty of a favorite Parisian bistro. Big cold artichokes are stuffed with layers of vegetables and shrimp. Dessert is a refreshing lemon soufflé custard that is excellent hot or cold. Sip a cool Johannisberg Riesling or a Chablis, if you like. The calorie count on this spring-through-fall luncheon is about 400 per person, allowing for buttered slices of Verona Loaf.

Shrimp and Artichokes Richelieu

4   **large, cold, cooked artichokes**
1   **cup cooked baby peas, chilled**
1   **cup thinly sliced mushrooms**
    Tarragon Dressing (see below)
1   **cup sliced cooked carrots,**
    chilled
1   **cup cooked French-cut green**
    beans, chilled
½   **pound small cooked shrimp**
    Butter lettuce
    Cherry tomatoes

With your fingertips, reach into the artichokes and pull out the center prickly leaves; finish scraping them out with a spoon. Spoon a layer of peas in the center of each. Toss mushrooms in a few tablespoons of the dressing and place them on peas. Layer the carrots and beans and top with shrimp. Drizzle the remaining dressing over all. Serve on plates lined with butter lettuce and garnish with cherry tomatoes. Makes 4 servings, about 215 calories each.

Tarragon Dressing: Mix together 2 tablespoons olive oil, 3 tablespoons white wine vinegar, 2 teaspoons Dijon mustard, ¼ teaspoon salt, freshly ground pepper to taste, 1 tablespoon chopped fresh parsley, and 1 teaspoon chopped fresh tarragon (or ¼ teaspoon dried tarragon).

Lemon Soufflé Custard

- 2 tablespoons flour
- 6 tablespoons sugar
- 3 tablespoons nonfat dry milk
- 4 eggs, separated
- 1½ teaspoons freshly grated lemon peel
- 4 tablespoons lemon juice
- 1 cup water
- ¼ teaspoon salt
- ¼ teaspoon cream of tartar

Mix together the flour, 4 tablespoons of the sugar, and the milk powder. In a different bowl beat egg yolks until thick, then add the sugar-flour mixture. Stir in the grated lemon peel, the lemon juice, and the water. Beat egg whites until foamy, then add salt and cream of tartar and beat until stiff but not dry; beat in the remaining 2 tablespoons sugar. Fold this meringue into the egg yolk mixture. Spoon into buttered individual soufflé dishes or other small baking dishes. Place in a pan containing 1 inch of hot water and bake in a 350° oven for 20 to 25 minutes, or until set. ☆ Makes 6 servings, about 120 calories each.

☆ Make a day in advance and serve chilled.

Pacific Salad Luncheon Serves 6

Spinach-Wrapped Sesame Chicken
Green Bean, Mushroom, and Shrimp Salad
Mango Sherbet
Jasmine Tea

Flavor overtones of the Pacific influence this festive salad luncheon. It is ideal for hot weather midday dining or for a late supper. Prelude the meal with spinach-wrapped chicken morsels dipped in a sesame yogurt sauce. A marinated green bean and mushroom salad ringed with seafood is the focal point. Oriental sesame seed wafers would add a nice crispy texture. An exotic mango ice, punctuated with lime, is a cool finale. A Sauvignon Blanc or a dry Chenin Blanc would be a delightful accompaniment. The total calorie count for this summer lunch is about 375 per person.

Spinach-Wrapped Sesame Chicken

1   pound chicken breasts
½   cup chicken stock (see next page)
2   teaspoons soy sauce
    Few drops sesame oil
1   bunch spinach
¾   cup plain yogurt
    Salt
    Freshly ground pepper
1   tablespoon toasted sesame
        seeds

Simmer chicken breasts in stock along with soy sauce and sesame oil, cooking just until tender, about 15 minutes. Drain and let the meat cool. Remove skin and bones and cut the meat into strips approximately 1½ by ½ inches. Blanch spinach in boiling salted water for 30 seconds; drain, rinse under cold running water, and drain again. Discard the stems. Wrap each piece of chicken in a spinach leaf and arrange on a platter. Stir together the yogurt, salt, pepper, and sesame seeds and spoon into a bowl. Set out a small container of toothpicks, to dip the appetizers in the sauce. Makes 6 servings, about 125 calories each.

Chicken Stock: Place in a large kettle 3 to 4 pounds of chicken necks and wings, 1½ quarts water, 2 teaspoons salt, 1 peeled and quartered onion, 1 sliced stalk celery, and 1 peeled and halved carrot. Cover and simmer 1 hour. Remove chicken parts, strain stock, and chill. Skim fat when cool. Freeze stock for other dishes.

Green Bean, Mushroom, and Shrimp Salad

1	pound green beans, French-cut
1	pound mushrooms, sliced
1	red onion, sliced into thin rings
½	cup sliced water chestnuts or jicama
⅓	cup olive oil
⅓	cup red wine vinegar
1	tablespoon Dijon mustard
½	teaspoon crumbled dried oregano
1	teaspoon salt
⅛	teaspoon pepper
1	clove garlic, minced
	Salad greens
¾	pound cooked medium shrimp, mussels, or scallops
1	hard-cooked egg yolk
2	tablespoons chopped fresh parsley

Cook the beans in boiling salted water to cover for 5 to 7 minutes, or until crisp tender. Drain and rinse under cold running water. Place them in a bowl and add the mushrooms, onion rings, and water chestnuts. Mix together the oil, vinegar, mustard, oregano, salt, pepper, and garlic. Pour this over the vegetables and mix lightly. Chill 1 hour. Arrange on a platter lined with the greens and ring with your choice of cooked seafood. Sieve the egg yolk over the top and sprinkle with parsley. Makes 6 servings, about 175 calories each.

Mango Sherbet

2 medium mangos
1 cup orange juice
  Juice of 1 lime
3 tablespoons honey
2 egg whites
  Mint sprigs or flower blossoms

Peel and halve mangos, scoop out the seeds, and dice fruit. Place in a blender or food processor with the orange juice, lime juice, and honey. Purée until smooth. Pour into a shallow pan or ice cube tray and freeze until firm. Remove from freezer and spoon into a food processor. Using the steel blade attachment, process until light and slushy. (Without a processor, beat with an electric mixer.) Beat egg whites until soft peaks form; fold into fruit. Spoon into a freezer container, cover, and freeze until firm. ☆ Serve in dessert bowls or wine glasses, garnished with a sprig of mint or a blossom. Makes 6 servings, about 75 calories each.

☆ The sherbet may remain frozen for 2 weeks.

Crab Season Luncheon Serves 6

Watercress Soup
Crab and Citrus Vinaigrette Salad
Frozen Lemon Shells

An interplay of flavors—the spicy bite of watercress, the zest of citrus, and the refreshing tone of frozen lemon yogurt—characterizes this warm weather luncheon. If fresh crab meat is out of season, let small cooked shrimp, poached scallops, or mussels stand in. A Fumé Blanc or Sauvignon Blanc would enhance the meal. Allow 460 calories per person for this pretty luncheon.

Watercress Soup

1   medium onion, chopped
1   teaspoon butter
4   new (red) potatoes, diced
4   cups chicken stock (see
       page 26)
1   clove garlic, minced
1   teaspoon salt
¼   teaspoon white pepper
1   large bunch watercress, stems
       removed and leaves chopped
1   tablespoon cornstarch
1   tablespoon cold water
¼   cup chopped fresh parsley
½   cup plain yogurt

Sauté the onion in butter in a large saucepan, cooking until glazed. Add the potatoes, chicken stock, garlic, salt, and pepper. Cover and simmer until tender, about 15 minutes. Add the watercress and simmer 2 minutes longer. Blend together the cornstarch and cold water and stir in; cook until thickened. Process in a food processor in batches with parsley and blend in the yogurt. ☆ Makes 6 servings, about 40 calories each.

☆ Prepare in advance to this point and refrigerate. Reheat or serve cold.

Crab and Citrus Vinaigrette Salad

1   large head butter lettuce, washed and torn into bite-sized pieces

2   pink grapefruit, peeled and sectioned

2   oranges, peeled and sliced or sectioned

1   pound cooked crab meat

1   medium avocado, diced

⅓   cup safflower oil

1½ tablespoons lemon juice

1½ tablespoons white wine vinegar

1   teaspoon freshly grated lemon peel

1   teaspoon Dijon mustard

1   shallot or green onion, finely chopped

½   teaspoon salt
     Freshly ground pepper

3   tablespoons toasted slivered almonds or chopped filberts

Place in a large salad bowl the lettuce, grapefruit, oranges, crab meat, and avocado. Shake together the oil, lemon juice, vinegar, lemon peel, mustard, shallot, salt, and pepper to taste. Pour this dressing over the salad just before serving and mix well. Sprinkle with nuts. Makes 6 servings, about 290 calories each.

Frozen Lemon Shells

6   lemons

1½ pints lemon or raspberry frozen yogurt

Slice off the tops of the lemons one-third of the way down. Slice off just enough of the other end to make a firm base for the shell to stand upright. Squeeze the juice from the fruit, saving the juice for another purpose and keeping the shells intact. Pack each shell with frozen yogurt. Top with lemon peel caps and freeze, covered, until firm. Serve on lemon-leaf-lined plates. Makes 6 servings, about 130 calories each.

A Tuscany Luncheon _Serves 6_

Italian Tri-Color Salad
Spinach and Sausage Frittata
Verona Loaf (see page 8)
Fruit Compote

This Italian luncheon is easy on the cook. The frittata may be made in advance and reheated; it is also excellent served cold. The bread may come from the freezer. The tomato salad and fruit dessert are put together in minutes. A dry French Colombard or Gewürztraminer would spark the entrée. The calorie count for this indoor or outdoor luncheon is about 480 per person.

Italian Tri-Color Salad

4 large beefsteak tomatoes
2 ounces Mozzarella cheese, thinly sliced
12 fresh basil leaves
Sea salt
Freshly ground pepper
2 tablespoons red wine vinegar

Peel and slice tomatoes and arrange on a platter. Overlap cheese slices on tomatoes and cluster basil in the center. Grind salt and pepper to taste over all and drizzle with vinegar. Makes 6 servings, about 50 calories each.

Spinach and Sausage Frittata

2 lean, mild Italian sausages (about 6 ounces)
1 teaspoon butter
1 bunch green onions or 1 large white onion, finely chopped
2 large bunches spinach, finely chopped, or 3 packages (10 ounces) frozen chopped spinach, thawed and drained
6 eggs
½ cup sausage broth

½ teaspoon salt
¼ teaspoon freshly ground pepper
1½ cups freshly grated Parmesan cheese
¼ cup chopped fresh parsley
1 tablespoon chopped fresh basil (or ¾ teaspoon dried basil)
3 cloves garlic, finely minced
¼ cup sunflower seeds

Poach the sausages in water to cover for 15 minutes. Drain, reserving ½ cup of the liquid, and let sausages cool slightly. Heat a large frying pan over medium-high heat, add butter and onions and sauté, stirring, until onions are limp; turn into a bowl. Add the uncooked spinach to onions and stir for 30 to 60 seconds, just until spinach wilts. Beat eggs until blended and add reserved sausage broth and salt and pepper to taste. Pour this over the vegetables and mix in the cheese, parsley, basil, and garlic. Dice sausages and stir the pieces in. Turn into a buttered 9 by 13-inch baking pan. Sprinkle with seeds. Bake in a 350° oven for 25 to 30 minutes, or until set. Serve hot or cold. Makes 6 servings, about 255 calories each.

Fruit Compote

3   peaches
2   cups seedless grapes
2   cups watermelon balls
2   cups honeydew melon balls
2   tablespoons orange liqueur
    Mint leaves

Peel and slice peaches into a bowl and mix in the grapes and melon balls. Spoon liqueur over fruit and chill briefly. Spoon into large-bowled wine glasses or stemmed sundae dishes. Garnish with mint sprigs. Makes 6 servings, about 75 calories each.

A Burgundy Party Luncheon Serves 12

Pickled Carrots
Ratatouille-Stuffed Crêpes
Sausage-Striped Veal and Pork Terrine
Peaches Flambé

Here is a party meal in a French mood. It suits a summer buffet luncheon or supper for a crowd. Designed for make-ahead preparation, the menu goes to the table with ease. The spread encompasses hot stuffed crêpes, a chilled veal and pork terrine (a cold meat loaf) ribboned with sausage, and sprightly pickled carrots—all to be done a day or two in advance. The raspberry-glazed whole peaches, studded with almonds, are swiftly flambéed at the last minute. A White Zinfandel or Tavel Rosé would fill the wine role nicely. The calorie count for this luncheon is about 455 per person. If desired, add a salad of butter lettuce and watercress (see page 54) and a fresh Verona Loaf (see page 8) which will add another 185 calories.

Pickled Carrots

1¼ cups white vinegar
⅓ cup sugar
1¼ teaspoons salt
1½ teaspoons celery seed
1 tablespoon mustard seed
 Few black peppercorns
10 carrots, peeled and cut into
 slender sticks

In a saucepan, combine the vinegar, sugar, salt, celery and mustard seed, and peppercorns and bring to a boil. Add the carrot sticks. Simmer until crisp tender and chill in the sauce. ☆ Drain and serve in a crock. Makes 12 servings, about 30 calories each.

☆ These keep at least 1 week in the refrigerator.

Ratatouille-Stuffed Crêpes

12 crêpes, 6-inch size (see next page)
1 small eggplant, peeled and cut into ¾-inch cubes
2 medium zucchini, sliced ⅛ inch thick
1 red pepper, seeded and cut into julienne strips
1 green pepper, seeded and cut into julienne strips
1 large onion, chopped
2 tablespoons olive oil
2 cloves garlic, minced

2 cans (1 pound) whole peeled or stewed tomatoes, coarsely chopped
½ teaspoon salt
¼ teaspoon freshly ground pepper
3 tablespoons minced fresh parsley
1 tablespoon chopped fresh basil, or ¾ teaspoon dried basil
1 cup freshly grated Parmesan cheese

Make the crêpes, stack and cover them, and keep warm until needed. Place the eggplant, zucchini, and peppers in a bowl, sprinkle with salt and let stand 1 hour. Pour off any juices that accumulate and rinse under cold running water. Sauté the onion in the oil, using a large frying pan, and cook until glazed. Add the garlic and the salted and rinsed vegetables and sauté a few minutes longer. Add the tomatoes, salt, and pepper and simmer for 10 minutes, covered. Uncover and cook about 10 minutes more, until sauce is thickened and vegetables are just tender. Season with parsley, basil, and ½ cup of the cheese. Lay out one crêpe and spoon a ribbon of vegetable mixture down the center. Roll up and place in a greased shallow baking dish. Repeat with remaining crêpes. ☆ Sprinkle with the remaining ½ cup cheese and heat in a 375° oven for 15 minutes, or until hot. Makes 12 servings, about 125 calories each.

☆ Prepare in advance to this point and refrigerate.

Crêpes: In a blender container, mix 3 eggs, ¼ cup powdered milk, ¼ cup cornstarch, ¾ cup water, and ½ teaspoon salt. Pour about 3 tablespoons batter into a lightly buttered hot crêpe pan and cook until browned underneath. Remove from pan and repeat with remaining batter. ☆ Makes about 12 crêpes, 6 to 7 inches in diameter, about 40 calories each.

☆ Prepare crêpes 2 to 3 days in advance to this point and chill, stacked and covered. They may also be frozen, with waxed paper layered between them.

Sausage-Striped Veal and Pork Terrine

2 mild Italian sausages	½ teaspoon allspice
1 large onion, chopped	½ teaspoon Dijon-style dry mustard
2 tablespoons dry sherry	
1 pound ground veal	¼ teaspoon ginger
1 pound ground pork	¼ teaspoon cloves
1 egg	¼ teaspoon white pepper
1 egg white	Freshly ground pepper
⅓ cup sausage or chicken stock (see page 26)	⅓ cup nonfat dry milk
2 teaspoons salt	2 bay leaves
	6 peppercorns

Poach the sausages in water to cover for 15 minutes; cool. Turn onion into a dry frying pan and heat over moderately high heat, stirring, until limp. Pour in sherry and scrape the pan. Turn into a bowl. Add the ground veal and pork, egg, egg white, stock, salt, allspice, mustard, ginger, cloves, the white pepper, black pepper to taste, and the powdered milk; mix lightly. Turn half of the mixture into a greased 9 by 5-inch loaf pan. Arrange the whole sausages in a line down the center. Cover with the remaining meat mixture and garnish with bay leaves and peppercorns. Cover with foil. Place in a pan containing 1 inch of hot water and bake in a 350° oven for 1 hour. Remove foil and continue baking for 1 hour longer. Cool and chill 1 day before serving. ☆ Makes 12 servings, about 220 calories each.

☆ The terrine keeps up to 5 days, refrigerated. For best results do not freeze.

Peaches Flambé

12 peaches
 5 tablespoons raspberry jelly
 3 tablespoons very finely chopped
      blanched almonds
½ cup dark rum

Dip the peaches in boiling water for 30 seconds, then dip in cold water and slip off the skins. Melt jelly in a large frying pan or chafing dish. Place peaches in the pan, coat with jelly, and sprinkle almonds over them. When ready to serve, warm the rum, ignite 1 tablespoonful, and spoon it over the peaches. Gradually add the remaining rum, letting the fruit flame. Makes 12 servings, about 80 calories each.

Harvest Luncheon Serves 8

Stuffed Beefsteak Tomatoes
Spinach and Hot Chicken Liver Salad
Apple Nut Crisp

Scarlet tomato shells filled with a succulent lamb mixture make a regal entrée for an autumn luncheon. Accompany with a spinach and pine nut salad and follow with hot apple crisp. Consider a Gamay or Grignolino Rosé to sip with the meal. The calorie count for this menu is about 435 per person.

Stuffed Beefsteak Tomatoes

8	large tomatoes
	Salt
2	large onions, chopped
3	carrots, peeled and chopped
3	cloves garlic, minced
1	teaspoon butter
2	tablespoons chopped fresh parsley
1	pound ground lamb
1	teaspoon salt
1	teaspoon allspice
	Freshly ground pepper
½	cup chicken broth (see page 26)
2	tablespoons freshly grated Parmesan cheese

With a small paring knife cut the core from the tomatoes. Slice off a lid, cutting about ¼ inch from the top. With a knife or a spoon scoop the inner tomato portion into a bowl and chop it into small pieces. Lightly salt the inner tomato shell. Using a large frying pan, sauté the onions, carrots, and garlic in butter until glazed, about 10 minutes. Turn into a bowl and mix in the parsley, lamb, salt, allspice, pepper to taste, broth, and the chopped tomatoes. Pack this mixture into the tomato shells and sprinkle with cheese. Cover each with a tomato lid and place in a baking dish. Bake in a 350° oven for 1¼ hours. ☆ Makes 8 servings, about 175 calories each.

☆ Prepare in advance to this point and refrigerate. Reheat to serve.

Spinach and Hot Chicken Liver Salad

3 large bunches spinach (about
   3 pounds)
¼ cup olive oil
2 tablespoons red wine vinegar
2 tablespoons dry red wine
1 tablespoon lemon juice
2 teaspoons Dijon mustard

1 shallot, minced
½ teaspoon salt
8 chicken livers
1 teaspoon butter
3 tablespoons lightly toasted pine
   nuts or roasted sunflower
   seeds
Freshly ground pepper

Wash the spinach leaves well, discarding stems, and tear into bite-sized pieces. Wrap in paper towels, slip into a plastic bag, and chill. Just before serving, mix together well the oil, vinegar, wine, lemon juice, mustard, shallot, and salt. Place spinach in a bowl, pour on the dressing, and mix lightly. Sauté the livers in butter, cooking until still pink inside. Spoon spinach salad onto plates and garnish each with a hot chicken liver. Sprinkle with the nuts and a little ground pepper. Makes 6 servings, about 100 calories each.

Apple Nut Crisp

8 large cooking apples
⅓ cup (packed) brown sugar
⅓ cup chopped filberts or
   slivered almonds

1½ teaspoons freshly grated orange
   peel
2 tablespoons melted butter

Peel, core, and slice the apples and arrange them in a greased 9-inch baking pan. Mix together the sugar, nuts, orange peel, and butter and sprinkle over the top. Bake in a 375° oven for 30 to 40 minutes, or until apples are tender when pierced with a fork. ☆ Serve warm or at room temperature. Makes 6 servings, about 160 calories each.

☆ Prepare in advance to this point and reheat, if desired.

Parisian Bistro Lunch Serves 6

Les Halles Onion Soup
Bistro Salad
Pears in Red Wine

For a bistro-style lunch, offer cheese-crusted bowls of steaming French onion soup, a crisp apple and buttery avocado salad, and ruby wine-bathed pears for dessert. A Beaujolais or Barbera would complement the menu. The calorie count is about 445 per person for this French luncheon.

Les Halles Onion Soup

4	large onions, thinly sliced
1	tablespoon butter
1½	quarts beef stock (see below) or bouillon cubes plus water
2	cloves garlic, minced
¼	cup dry sherry
1½	cups freshly grated Gruyère or Monterey jack cheese

Using a large soup kettle, slowly sauté onions in butter until golden brown and caramelized, about 20 minutes, stirring occasionally. Add the stock and garlic and simmer for 30 minutes. Add the sherry and heat thoroughly. ☆ Ladle into ovenproof soup bowls and sprinkle with cheese. If desired, place under the broiler until cheese melts and browns. Makes 6 servings, about 160 calories each.

☆ Prepare in advance to this point and refrigerate. Reheat soup in a saucepan before broiling.

Beef Stock: Place 3 to 4 pounds of raw meaty beef bones in a roasting pan and roast in a 450° oven for 20 to 30 minutes, or until browned. If you like, roast 1 veal knuckle also. Transfer to a soup kettle. Add 2 chopped onions, 1 chopped carrot, 1 stalk chopped celery, a few celery leaves, a tied cheesecloth bag containing 1 bay leaf, 1 teaspoon thyme, a few sprigs parsley, and 2 cloves garlic. Pour in water to cover and add salt to taste. Simmer partially covered for 3 to 4 hours, skimming off the foam, and adding more water if necessary. Strain, skim the fat, and refrigerate or freeze until needed.

Bistro Salad

2 **heads butter lettuce**	1 **small avocado**
1 **bunch watercress**	2 **tablespoons sunflower seeds, or**
Wine Vinegar Dressing	**coarsely chopped toasted**
(see below)	**filberts or almonds**
1 **tart red apple**	

Tear lettuce into bite-sized pieces and place in a salad bowl; add the watercress leaves. Pour in the dressing and mix well. Halve, core, and slice the apple; peel and slice the avocado. Alternate apple and avocado in a pinwheel pattern on the salad greens. Sprinkle with sunflower seeds. Makes 6 servings, about 140 calories each.

Wine Vinegar Dressing: Mix together 4 tablespoons safflower oil, 3 tablespoons red wine vinegar, 2 teaspoons Dijon mustard, salt and freshly ground pepper to taste, and 1 teaspoon chopped fresh tarragon (or ¼ teaspoon crumbled dried tarragon).

Pears in Red Wine

6 **firm Bartlett, Anjou, or Bosc**	4 **thin slices lemon**
pears	1½ **cups dry red wine***
6 **whole cloves**	¼ **cup sugar**
2 **sticks cinnamon**	

Remove cores from the blossom end of the pears and slice off a little of the bottom evenly, so that pears stand upright, leaving the stems in place and the peels intact. Combine in a Dutch oven or baking pan the cloves, cinnamon, lemon slices, wine, and sugar; bring to a boil. Arrange the fruit in a baking pan, stem up, and pour in the sauce. Cover and bake in a 400° oven for 20 minutes. Remove cover and continue baking 20 to 25 minutes longer, basting occasionally, until fruit is tender. ☆ Serve hot or cold. Makes 6 servings, about 145 calories each.

☆ Prepare in advance to this point and reheat, if desired.

* If desired, substitute apple juice for the wine.

Picnics Anywhere

Golden Odyssey Picnic • French Wine Country
Picnic • Continental Picnic • Indian Summer
Tailgate Picnic • Napa Valley Wine Country
Picnic • Alsatian Country Picnic

Golden Odyssey Picnic Serves 8

Sprouted Lamb Loaves
Pocket Bread Peasant Salad
Fruit Basket

Transpose the intriguing elements of a Turkish picnic for a charming Western alfresco spread. Here individual lamb loaves and pocket sandwiches filled with a cool salad refresh a midday gathering. Let the season's fruit bounty be the juicy-sweet finale. A White or Rosé Cabernet Sauvignon would be a fine choice. The calorie count for this outdoor spread is about 450 per person, allowing 50 calories for the fruit.

Sprouted Lamb Loaves

1   large onion, finely chopped
1½ pounds lean ground lamb
½   pound lean ground veal or pork
⅓   cup toasted wheat germ
1   cup chopped alfalfa sprouts
½   cup chicken or beef stock (see
     page 26 or page 38)
2   eggs
3   tablespoons chopped fresh
     parsley
1   teaspoon freshly grated orange
     peel
2   cloves garlic, minced
1½ teaspoons salt
     Freshly ground pepper
1   teaspoon crumbled dried
     oregano

Sauté onion in a dry frying pan over medium-low heat, stirring until glazed; turn into a bowl. Mix in all remaining ingredients, just until blended. Pat mixture into greased muffin pans. Bake in a 375° oven for 20 to 25 minutes, or until lightly browned and completely cooked. ☆ Serve hot or cold. Makes 8 servings, allowing 2 loaves apiece, about 290 calories each.

☆ May be prepared 1 or 2 days in advance.

Pocket Bread Peasant Salad

 1 cucumber, peeled and sliced
 1 bunch green onions, chopped
1½ cups cherry tomatoes, halved
 1 green pepper, seeded and diced
 1 red pepper, seeded and diced
12 Mediterranean olives, pitted
    and chopped
 2 ounces feta cheese, crumbled
 1 inner head Romaine or other
    salad greens, torn into
    bite-sized bits
    Lemon Dressing (see below)
 4 pita or pocket breads, cut in
    half
 ½ cup plain yogurt

Combine in a bowl (or plastic container for easy carrying) the cucumber, onions, tomatoes, peppers, olives, cheese, and Romaine. Just before serving, pour on the dressing and mix lightly. Spoon into split pita bread, adding a dollop of yogurt. Makes 8, about 110 calories each.

Lemon Dressing: Mix together 2 tablespoons lemon juice, 2 tablespoons chopped fresh parsley, ½ teaspoon salt, ½ teaspoon crumbled oregano, and freshly ground pepper to taste.

French Wine Country Picnic *Serves 8*

Potage Fermier
Pistachio-Studded Chicken Terrine
Artichokes with Caviar and Yogurt
Strawberries with Cassis

A French country picnic makes an apropos repast for a holiday outing. The menu lends itself to advance preparation and is easy to tote to an ocean or mountain setting. It begins with a flavor-packed vegetable soup called potage fermier, which means farmer's garden soup. It is excellent hot, carried in a wide-mouthed thermos. Or plan to purée it and serve it chilled. A pistachio-dotted chicken and pork terrine is the entrée. Prepare it a day or two in advance, as ample chilling mellows the flavors. Cold whole artichokes, filled with yogurt and caviar, make a choice accompaniment. Fresh strawberries splashed with crème de cassis (a black currant liqueur) provide a light and refreshing finale. As a picnic wine, consider one of the new White Zinfandels or a Gamay Beaujolais. The calorie count totals 400 per person for this holiday picnic.

Potage Fermier

1 medium onion, finely chopped	½ teaspoon crumbled dried tarragon
1 teaspoon butter	½ teaspoon salt
1½ quarts chicken stock (see page 26)	Freshly ground pepper
2 medium potatoes, peeled and diced	2 tablespoons finely chopped fresh parsley
1 bunch leeks, sliced	½ cup grated Parmesan or Romano cheese

Using a large saucepot, sauté the onion in butter until soft. Add the stock and potatoes; cover and simmer 15 minutes. Add the leeks, tarragon, salt, and pepper to taste; cover and simmer 10 minutes longer. Mash with a potato masher or purée in a blender. ☆ Serve hot or cold, garnished with parsley and cheese. Makes 8 servings, about 65 calories each.

☆ Prepare 1 or 2 days in advance to this point.

Pistachio-Studded Chicken Terrine

1 large onion, finely chopped	¼ teaspoon pepper
2 teaspoons butter	1 egg
1 pound lean boneless pork	1 egg white
1½ pounds (4 large) chicken breasts, split, boned, and skinned	⅓ cup nonfat dry milk
	⅓ cup chicken stock (see page 26)
2 teaspoons salt	2 tablespoons dry sherry
½ teaspoon dried thyme	2 cloves garlic, minced
½ teaspoon allspice	6 tablespoons pistachios
½ teaspoon freshly grated lemon peel	2 bay leaves
	6 peppercorns
¼ teaspoon nutmeg	

Sauté the onion in butter until limp. Grind the pork and chicken in a food processor or food grinder. Add the next 6 seasonings, the egg, egg white, powdered milk, chicken stock, sherry, and garlic. Mix until blended and spread half of the mixture in a greased 8 by 4½-inch loaf pan. Sprinkle with half the pistachios. Cover with the remaining meat mixture and sprinkle with the remaining nuts. Decorate the top with bay leaves and peppercorns. Cover with foil. Place in a pan containing 1 inch of water and bake in a 325° oven for 2 hours, or until set. Remove from water and chill 1 day before serving. ☆ Makes 12 servings, about 210 calories each.

☆ The terrine may be refrigerated for 5 days.

Artichokes with Caviar and Yogurt

8 large artichokes
1 tablespoon salad oil
½ cup yogurt
3 tablespoons caviar

Cut off the stems of the artichokes to make a flat base. Pull off the outer leaves and then, with kitchen shears, cut off the thorns from the remaining leaves. Cook in boiling salted water with the oil for 40 minutes, or just until tender. Drain and chill. At serving time, pull out the center leaves and scoop out the fuzzy portion underneath. Spoon 1 tablespoon plain yogurt inside each cavity and top with a teaspoon of caviar. Makes 8 servings, about 65 calories each.

Strawberries with Cassis

1½ quarts strawberries
⅓ cup crème de cassis liqueur or
     syrup

Wash the berries just before serving and mound in a wicker basket. If desired, leave stems on. Serve the crème de cassis in a small bowl for dipping. An alternative is to halve or slice the berries and serve them in individual bowls with the liqueur poured on top. Makes 8 servings, about 60 calories each.

Continental Picnic Serves 8

Curried Green Pea Soup
Cucumber-Stuffed Tomatoes
Marinated Salmon Bistro-Style
Blackberries with Coeur à la Crème

*A menu that adapts easily to a portable feast is nice to have in your sum-
mer repertoire. And make-ahead dishes are an extra bonus. These
specialties can be made at least a day or two in advance. Packed in an
insulated container, each one travels well. The flavor emphasis here is
basically French, with seasoning subtleties borrowed from Scandinavia
and India. The starter is a pretty pale green soup spiced with curry, excellent hot or cold. The entrée features thinly sliced salmon, which actually
"cooks" in a vinegar and wine marinade that pickles the onion rings as
well. It is a renowned favorite of a certain Parisian bistro. Sprightly
cucumber slices in tomato shells enhance the main course. A hint of
liqueur scents the sleek cottage cheese mold that forms a rich-tasting but
lean backdrop to the season's sweet, juicy blackberries. A California
Chardonnay or a French Meursault would be appropriate. The calorie
count for this meal is about 530 calories per person.*

Curried Green Pea Soup

1 teaspoon curry powder	3 cups chicken broth (see page 26)
1 teaspoon butter	1 package (10 ounces) frozen baby peas
1 large leek (white part only) chopped	½ teaspoon salt
2 shallots or green onions, chopped	White pepper
1 medium potato, peeled and diced	½ cup plain yogurt
	Chopped fresh chives

Using a large saucepan or soup pot, sauté the curry powder in butter for
1 minute, stirring. Add the leek and shallots and sauté until the vegetables
are soft. If desired, cover the pan so that the vegetables steam slightly.
Add the potato and broth and simmer 15 minutes. Add the peas, salt, and
pepper to taste and boil 1 minute. (Avoid overcooking to retain color.)
Purée with the yogurt in a blender or food processor. Ladle into bowls and
garnish with chives. If desired, serve cold. Makes 8 servings, about 55
calories each.

Cucumber-Stuffed Tomatoes

3 large cucumbers
¼ cup white wine vinegar
1 tablespoon water
2 tablespoons sugar
¼ teaspoon salt
  Freshly ground pepper
¼ teaspoon dried dill
2 tablespoons chopped fresh
    parsley
2 tablespoons chopped chives
8 medium tomatoes
  Butter lettuce or watercress

Leave peel on 1 of the cucumbers and peel the other 2, then thinly slice *all* cucumbers. Sprinkle generously with salt and let stand 15 minutes for water to exude. Rinse under cold running water to remove the salt. Mix together in a bowl the vinegar, water, sugar, salt, pepper to taste, and dill. Add the cucumber slices, cover, and chill at least 4 hours. At serving time, drain off juices and mix in the parsley and chives. Core the tomatoes and cut into wedges, slicing almost to the bottom. Place each tomato on a plate lined with lettuce or watercress and fill the center with pickled cucumber slices. Makes 8 servings, about 50 calories each.

Marinated Salmon Bistro-Style

2 pounds salmon fillets
1 tablespoon salt
1½ tablespoons sugar
½ teaspoon freshly ground
    pepper
3 medium onions, thinly sliced
2 lemons, thinly sliced
½ cup lemon juice
½ cup white wine vinegar
½ cup dry white wine

Slice salmon very thinly across the grain into approximately 1½ by 3-inch pieces (the fish slices more easily if slightly frozen). Mix together in a bowl the salt, sugar, and pepper. Dip fish slices in the dry ingredients, lightly coating both sides. Place a layer of onions and lemons in the bottom of a baking dish or other glass or porcelain container. Add a layer of salmon. Repeat, alternating onions, lemons, and fish. Mix together the lemon juice, vinegar, and white wine and pour over all. Cover and chill at least 1 day, basting several times with the juices. Keeps refrigerated for 4 to 5 days. Serve both salmon slices and onion rings. Makes 8 servings, about 300 calories each.

Blackberries with Coeur à la Crème

1   cup large-curd cottage cheese
4   ounces cream cheese
1   tablespoon sour cream
1   tablespoon orange or cherry
        liqueur
1   teaspoon powdered sugar
1   quart blackberries,
        strawberries, or raspberries

Place in a food processor fitted with a steel blade the cottage cheese, cream cheese, sour cream, liqueur, and sugar. Blend until smooth. Turn into a 1-pint mold (such as a charlotte mold) or into a heart-shaped wicker basket mold, either lined with cheesecloth. Cover and chill overnight. To serve, unmold, peel off the cheesecloth, and surround with berries. ☆ Serve a wedge of cheese and a spoonful of fruit on dessert plates, with forks. Makes 8 servings, about 125 calories each.

☆ The cheese mold may be prepared 2 to 3 days in advance to this point.

Indian Summer Tailgate Picnic *Serves 6*

Currant-Glazed Game Hens
Harvest Salad
Coffee Ice Cream with Cointreau
Espresso with Cognac

This flexible luncheon is ideal for either a portable tailgate picnic or an indoor repast. Roast the ruby-glazed game hens well in advance. The salad, embellished with fruit, seeds, nuts, and cheese, is almost a meal in itself. Dessert can vary with the locale. Present ice cream splashed with a favorite liqueur (the combination below is excellent) if at home; offer hot brewed espresso laced with cognac if away. Tote a chilled Gewürztraminer or Alsatian Riesling, if you like. Allow about 480 calories for the lunch with ice cream; 345 for the alternative.

Currant-Glazed Game Hens

3   **Rock Cornish game hens**
½   **cup minced fresh parsley**
2   **teaspoons fresh tarragon,**
      or ½ teaspoon crumbled
      dried tarragon
1   **tablespoon butter**
½   **teaspoon salt**
3   **tablespoons red currant jelly**
3   **tablespoons brandy or cognac**

Remove giblets from hens, rinse in cold water, and pat dry. Mix the parsley and tarragon and tuck 2 tablespoons of the mixture inside each cavity. Rub outer surfaces with butter and place in a shallow roasting pan. Roast in a 375° oven for 30 minutes. Heat jelly and brandy until jelly melts. Brush over hens and roast 30 minutes longer, basting with glaze every 5 or 10 minutes. Remove from pan, cool, and chill. Cut in half to serve. Makes 6 servings, about 180 calories each.

Harvest Salad

1 head butter, red, or
    Australian lettuce
1 Bartlett pear
1 sweet red pepper
1 tart red apple
    Wine Vinegar Dressing (see
    page 39)
¼ cup salted sunflower seeds or
    chopped toasted filberts
1 cup alfalfa sprouts
½ cup shredded Gruyère cheese

Tear lettuce into bite-sized pieces and place in a bowl. Dice the pear, pepper, and apple and add to the greens. Pour the dressing over all and mix lightly. Sprinkle with sunflower seeds, alfalfa sprouts, and cheese. Makes 6 servings, about 135 calories each.

Coffee Ice Cream with Cointreau

1½ pints coffee ice cream
2 tablespoons Cointreau or other
    liqueur

Just before serving, scoop ice cream into dessert bowls and drizzle 1 teaspoon liqueur on top of each scoop. Makes 6 servings, about 165 calories each.

Espresso with Cognac

Brew espresso and carry in a thermos container. Lace each serving with 1 teaspoon cognac.

Napa Valley Wine Country Picnic Serves 8

Zucchini Potage
Filbert Turkey Terrine
Butter Lettuce and Watercress Salad
Chocolate-Dipped Strawberries

Here is an easy, flexible French picnic that travels well on an outing or unfolds nicely in a garden setting at home. The starter is a remarkably rich-tasting yet lean zucchini soup with an enticing verdant color. (The secret is to shred the zucchini so that it cooks in minutes in the broth. This is a fine way to utilize the overgrown squash from your garden.) The entrée is a tasty terrine that slices easily. An oil-and-vinegar dressed salad refreshes it. Chocolate-dipped strawberries are the last delight to savor. For a wine, consider a new White Cabernet Sauvignon to match the entrée. This French-style summer picnic or supper contains approximately 440 calories per person.

Zucchini Potage

1	quart chicken stock (see page 26)	Salt
6	cups shredded zucchini	Freshly ground pepper
2	green onions, chopped	Chopped fresh chives or parsley
2	cloves garlic, chopped	

Bring the chicken stock to a boil. Add the zucchini*, onions, and garlic and simmer 5 minutes, uncovered, to retain the bright color. Puree in a blender and season with salt and pepper to taste. ☆ Ladle into bowls or mugs and sprinkle with chives. Makes 8 servings, about 25 calories each.

☆ Prepare a day or 2 in advance and serve hot or cold.

* If using the extra-large home-grown squash, first cut them in thick slices, salt lightly, and let them stand 15 minutes for the juices to exude. Then rinse and shred.

Filbert Turkey Terrine

1 large onion, finely chopped
1 teaspoon butter
1½ pounds turkey sausage
   (available in 12-ounce
   packages)
½ pound lean ground veal or pork
½ teaspoon salt
   Generous dash of freshly
   ground pepper
½ teaspoon dry mustard
½ teaspoon crumbled dried
   tarragon

1 teaspoon freshly grated lemon
   peel
2 tablespoons brandy or cognac
½ cup nonfat dry milk powder
1 egg
1 egg white
⅓ cup chicken stock (see page 26)
2 cloves garlic, minced
3 tablespoons filberts

Sauté onion in butter until limp and golden brown. Place in a large bowl all ingredients but the last one. Mix lightly just until blended. Reserve 6 nuts for garnish and mix in remaining nuts. Pat meat into a buttered 9 by 5-inch pan and top with a row of reserved nuts. Cover with foil. Place in a pan containing 1 inch of water. Bake in a 350° oven for 1 hour. Remove foil and continue baking 45 to 50 minutes longer or until set. Remove from water bath and chill at least 1 day before serving. Makes 8 servings, about 220 calories each.

☆ The terrine keeps 5 days in the refrigerator.

Butter Lettuce and Watercress Salad

4 tablespoons minced shallots
6 tablespoons olive or safflower
  oil
3 tablespoons red wine vinegar
1 tablespoon Dijon mustard
  Salt

Freshly ground pepper
1 cup watercress leaves, stems
  removed
2 large heads butter lettuce, torn
  into bite-sized pieces

Add shallots to oil and mix well with vinegar, mustard, and salt and pepper to taste. Place greens in a salad bowl, pour in the dressing, and mix lightly. Makes 8 servings, about 85 calories each.

Chocolate-Dipped Strawberries

4 ounces semisweet chocolate
4 teaspoons orange liqueur
2 tablespoons coffee
4 cups strawberries with stems,
  chilled

Melt chocolate with liqueur and coffee in a double boiler over hot—not boiling—water. (Or melt in a 300° oven for 10 minutes.) Stir to blend. Dip berries half way into the chocolate. Place on a foil-lined pan, stem down, and chill until chocolate sets. Serve on plates lined with grape or citrus leaves. Makes 8 servings, about 110 calories each.

Alsatian Country Picnic Serves 10

Veal Loaf Cordon Bleu
Mushrooms à la Grècque
Crudités with Tarragon Herb Dip
Berry Bowl in Riesling

This Continental picnic suits many occasions—a midday sail, an outing to the beach, or a day in the wine country. The menu revolves around a stuffed veal loaf, marinated mushrooms, and a basket of colorful vegetables dipped in a fresh tarragon sauce. For dessert, steep a berry medley in wine at the picnic site. A Pinot Noir Blanc offers a spicy accompaniment. A good white jug wine would also be appropriate. Allow about 515 calories per person for this easy, make-ahead picnic.

Veal Loaf Cordon Bleu

1	bunch green onions, chopped	2	cloves garlic, minced
2	slices sour dough French bread or ¼ cup wheat germ	6	tablespoons chopped fresh parsley
3	tablespoons dry sherry	1½	pounds ground veal
⅓	cup chicken broth (see page 26)	½	pound ground beef or pork
2	eggs, or 3 egg whites	1	cup shredded jarlsberg cheese (about 4 ounces)
1½	teaspoons salt		
	Freshly ground pepper	1	ounce prosciutto, thinly sliced
1	teaspoon dry mustard		

Sauté green onions in a dry frying pan over medium-low heat, stirring, until they are limp; set aside. Blend the bread or wheat germ, sherry, broth, eggs, salt, pepper to taste, mustard, garlic, and 3 tablespoons of the parsley together until smooth. Place the ground meats in a bowl and add the seasoning-bread mixture; mix until blended. In a greased 9 by 13-inch baking pan, pat out half the meat mixture into a rectangle about 6 by 10 inches. Mix together the sautéed onions, cheese, prosciutto, and the remaining 3 tablespoons parsley and sprinkle this over the rectangle. Pat out the remaining meat on a sheet of waxed paper, making another 6 by 10-inch rectangle. Lay this over the cheese and ham filling and press the edges of the meat layers together, forming a compact rounded loaf. Bake in a 350° oven for 1 hour. Serve hot or chilled. ☆ Makes 10 servings, about 275 calories each.

☆ The loaf keeps 3 to 4 days in the refrigerator.

Mushrooms à la Grècque

1 pound button mushrooms*
½ cup chicken stock (see page 26)
1 tablespoon olive oil
1½ tablespoons lemon juice
1½ tablespoons white wine vinegar
1 clove garlic, slivered
4 black peppercorns

½ teaspoon dried tarragon
⅛ teaspoon fennel seed
  Salt
  Freshly ground pepper
2 tablespoons chopped fresh
  parsley

Wash and drain the mushrooms. Bring to a boil the chicken stock, oil, lemon juice, vinegar, garlic, peppercorns, tarragon, fennel, and salt and pepper to taste. Add the mushrooms and simmer 3 to 4 minutes. Remove with a slotted spoon and place in a bowl. Boil down the juices until reduced to a thick sauce. Pour this over the mushrooms and chill. Sprinkle with parsley at serving time. Makes 10 servings, about 18 calories each.

* If desired, substitute zucchini for the mushrooms and basil for the tarragon. Slice the zucchini into ¼-inch rounds. This will yield about 22 calories per serving.

Crudités with Tarragon Herb Dip

⅓ cup crème fraîche (see next page)
⅔ cup plain yogurt
2 teaspoons finely chopped fresh
  tarragon
1 teaspoon chopped onion or
  shallot

1 clove garlic, minced
3 tablespoons finely chopped
  fresh parsley
  Salt
  Freshly ground pepper

Mix the crème fraîche with the yogurt, tarragon, onion, garlic, parsley, and salt and pepper to taste. Turn into a serving container, cover, and chill. At serving time, arrange assorted crisp raw vegetables (cherry tomatoes, cucumber fingers, pea pods, turnip wedges, carrot sticks, cauliflowerets, radish roses) in a nosegay on a platter or in a basket. Serve the Tarragon Herb Dip in a separate bowl. The dip has about 60 calories per tablespoon.

Crème Fraîche: Combine 1 cup heavy cream with ½ cup sour cream in a stainless steel saucepan, stirring to blend, and heat just to 80° or 85°. Remove from heat, cover, and let stand at room temperature for 12 hours or overnight, until very thick, then chill. The recipe makes 1½ cups and keeps for 2 to 3 weeks. About 50 calories per tablespoon.

Berry Bowl in Riesling

1 quart strawberries, hulled

1 cup raspberries or wild strawberries

1 cup blueberries

1 bottle Alsatian, Johannisberg Riesling (semisweet), California Alexandria, or Malvasia Blanca

Place the washed, drained berries in a large cylindrical glass container, such as a wide-mouthed jar, and pour in the wine. Let steep for 1 hour before serving. Or, if desired, spoon berries into wide-bowled wine glasses or dessert bowls and pour the wine in just before serving. Makes 10 servings, about 100 calories each.

Ultraeasy Dinners

Tuscany Dinner • Tahitian Dinner •
Dinner from Hydra • Far Eastern Dinner •
French Country Dinner • Portuguese
Fish Cafe Dinner • Barbecue from Rhodes •
Cantonese Dinner • Normandy Fish Dinner •
Dinner from Lyon • Pacific Barbecue •
Spanish Party Dinner • Dad's Splendid
Dinner

Tuscany Dinner *Serves 6*

Wine Broth
Artichokes Italian
Saltimbocca
Caesar Salad
Peaches and Blueberries in Port

The delectable flavors of Northern Italian cooking characterize this dinner. Light, refreshing, and zestily seasoned, the dishes rely on the fresh abundance of the season prepared with imagination. Lemon peel and a splash of wine gild the starting beef broth. Italian blue cheese and anchovies accent baby artichokes. Veal rolls are filled with Gruyère and prosciutto. The salad is a Caesar. And for dessert, summer fruits mellow in port. Consider a Johannisberg Riesling or a Soave to sip with this meal. Contains approximately 490 calories per person.

Wine Broth

- 1 quart beef stock (see page 38)
- 1 teaspoon lemon juice
- ½ teaspoon Worcestershire sauce
  Dash of liquid hot pepper seasoning
- ½ cup dry red wine or sherry
- 6 strips lemon peel (zest)

Combine in a saucepan the stock, lemon juice, Worcestershire, and pepper seasoning and bring to a boil. Add the wine, heat thoroughly, and ladle into small bowls or cups. Garnish with a twist of lemon. Makes 6 servings, about 25 calories each.

Artichokes Italian

- 1½ pounds baby artichokes, trimmed and halved, or 2 packages (8 ounces) frozen artichoke hearts
- 1½ teaspoons olive oil
- 1 clove garlic, minced
- 1 green onion, finely chopped
- 1½ teaspoons lemon juice
- ¼ cup crumbled Gorgonzola or blue cheese
- 6 rolled anchovy fillets with capers

Cook artichokes or hearts in boiling salted water until barely tender, allowing about 15 to 20 minutes for fresh or 5 to 7 minutes for frozen; drain well. Add the oil, garlic, and onion to the pan and heat, shaking the pan until artichokes are coated with the mixture. Sprinkle with lemon juice. Turn onto a serving dish, sprinkle with cheese, and garnish with anchovies. Makes 6 servings, about 60 calories each.

Saltimbocca

$1\frac{1}{2}$ **pounds veal, cut into 12 pieces**
       as for scallopini
    Salt
    Freshly ground pepper
    Crumbled dried oregano
  6 **slices prosciutto**
  3 **ounces Gruyère or Provolone**
      cheese, cut in strips
  2 **tablespoons butter**
$\frac{1}{3}$ **cup dry white wine or Marsala**

Season the meat generously with salt, pepper, and oregano and place half a slice of prosciutto on each. Add a strip of cheese, roll up, and fasten with a toothpick. ☆ Melt butter in a large frying pan, add the meat rolls, and brown on all sides. Remove to a warm platter. Add wine and bring to a boil, scraping up pan juices and reducing the liquid slightly. Spoon the sauce over the meat rolls. Makes 6 servings, about 215 calories each.

☆ Prepare in advance to this point and refrigerate.

Caesar Salad

1 large head Romaine, washed
  and crisped
1 egg
4 tablespoons olive oil
2 tablespoons lemon juice
2 tablespoons white wine vinegar
½ teaspoon salt
½ teaspoon Dijon-style dry
  mustard
  Freshly ground pepper
½ cup freshly grated Parmesan
  cheese
6 anchovy fillets, diced (optional)
1 slice French bread, cut into
  small cubes and toasted

Break salad greens into bite-sized pieces. With a wire whisk, beat the egg, oil, lemon juice, vinegar, salt, mustard, and pepper to taste just until blended. Pour this over the greens and mix lightly. Sprinkle with cheese, anchovies, and croutons. Makes 6 servings, about 130 calories each.

Peaches and Blueberries in Port

4 firm, ripe peaches
¼ cup ruby Port
2 tablespoons honey or brown
  sugar
1 cup blueberries

Scald the peaches and slip off the skins. Slice into a saucepan. Add Port and honey. Cover and simmer 3 to 4 minutes, or until just tender. Add blueberries and chill. Makes 6 servings, about 60 calories each.

$\mathcal{T}$ahitian $\mathcal{D}$inner Serves 6

Vegetable Clam Sip
Gingered Turbot and Pineapple Pacific-Style
Broiled Bananas
Spinach Sesame
Daiquiri Ice

A Tahitian-style menu offers a change of pace that is certain to pique and please tastebuds. This is an almost-instant menu to boot—it is very quickly assembled. Frosty clam broth, splashed with lime, is the starter. Ginger-glazed fish is the entrée, partnered with broiled fruit and sesame flavored spinach. A dry Semillon or Emerald Dry would make a choice wine companion. Contains about 385 calories per person.

Vegetable Clam Sip

1½ cups chilled vegetable juice cocktail	1 lime, cut in wedges
1½ cups chilled clam juice	2 teaspoons fresh chopped basil or chives

Combine the vegetable and clam juices and pour into wine glasses. Garnish each with a wedge of lime, slit and poked on the rim of each glass. Sprinkle herbs over each. Makes 6 servings, about 30 calories each.

Gingered Turbot and Pineapple Pacific-Style

1½ pounds turbot or sole fillets	1 green onion, chopped
3 tablespoons soy sauce	1 teaspoon chopped fresh peeled
2 tablespoons dry sherry	ginger root
2 tablespoons lemon juice	12 spears fresh pineapple

Cut fish into serving-sized pieces. Mix together the soy, sherry, lemon juice, onion, and ginger in a shallow dish. Place fish in the marinade and let stand 30 minutes, turning once. Lay a sheet of foil on a broiling pan and place the fish on it. Broil, again turning once, until golden brown on both sides. Dip pineapple in the marinade and broil at the last minute, just to heat. Makes 6 servings, about 200 calories each.

Broiled Bananas

3 bananas
½ teaspoon butter
    Cinnamon or nutmeg

Peel bananas and split in half lengthwise. Place on foil on a broiling pan. Brush with the melted butter and sprinkle with cinnamon or nutmeg. Broil until hot and lightly browned on the edges. Makes 6 servings, about 45 calories each.

Spinach Sesame

2 bunches spinach
1 tablespoon cider vinegar
1 tablespoon sugar
1 tablespoon soy sauce
1 teaspoon sesame oil
½ teaspoon prepared hot mustard
1 tablespoon toasted sesame
      seeds
6 cherry tomatoes

Trim stems from spinach, wash it well, and steam until just wilted and still bright green; drain well. Mix together the vinegar, sugar, soy, sesame oil, and mustard. Spoon spinach into small individual bowls, such as ramekins, and spoon the dressing on top. Sprinkle with sesame seeds. Cut each tomato like a blossom by cutting in wedges but not all the way through. Garnish each serving with a tomato flower. Makes 6 servings, about 45 calories each.

Daiquiri Ice

2   teaspoons freshly grated lime
    peel
6   tablespoons sugar
2   cups water
¼   cup lime juice
¼   cup dark rum
    Blossoms or mint sprigs

Mash lime peel with ½ teaspoon of the sugar to bring out the essential oils. Combine the remaining sugar with water in a saucepan; bring to a boil and simmer just until sugar is dissolved. Remove from heat and stir in lime juice, rum, and peel. Pour into a shallow 9-inch pan and freeze until solid. Spoon into a food processor or electric mixer and process until light and fluffy. Transfer to a plastic container and freeze until firm. ☆ Serve in wine glasses or dessert bowls and garnish with flowers or mint sprigs. Makes 6 servings, about 65 calories each.

☆   The ice may be kept frozen about 2 weeks.

Dinner from Hydra Serves 6

Meze: Greek Olives and Pistachios
Lamb Bandit-Style
Shepherd's Salad
Pears and Kasseri

The novelty of finding at each place setting a foil packet or paper bag steaming with goodness inside lends a charming surprise to a party dinner. Here the Greek way of cooking "bandit style," by sealing the meat and vegetables in a bag, makes a tantalizing entrée. First, however, pass around a plate of typical Greek appetizers, called meze, such as olives and pistachios. A fresh vegetable salad and sliced pears served with the firm white Greek cheese called Kasseri round out the meal. A Gamay Noir or Kokkineli would be an appropriate wine to serve. The calorie count for this dinner with a surprise is about 575 per person, allowing 25 for the appetizers.

Lamb Bandit-Style

6 loin lamb chops
1 teaspoon salt
1 teaspoon crumbled dried oregano
  Freshly ground pepper
2 cloves garlic, minced
6 small zucchini, halved lengthwise

6 small yellow crookneck squash, halved lengthwise
1 bunch green onions, chopped
2 ounces feta cheese
3 tablespoons lemon juice
2 tablespoons butter, melted

Season the chops with the salt, oregano, pepper to taste, and the garlic. Place each on a large doubled square of foil* and lay 2 zucchini halves and 2 crookneck halves on top. Scatter onions on top of the squash and crumble the cheese over all. Drizzle with lemon juice and butter and sprinkle lightly with extra salt and pepper. Double-fold the foil squares at top and sides; secure sides with paper clips. Place packets in a baking pan and bake in a 350° oven for 1 hour. To serve, place sealed packets on dinner plates. Makes 6 servings, about 275 calories each.

* Well-greased white paper bags, about 6 inches across at the bottom, may substitute for the foil packets. Cut off 3 inches from the tops of the bags first. Place filled bags on a baking pan and use a spatula to transfer bags to dinner plates.

Shepherd's Salad

1 green pepper, seeded and
   thinly sliced
1 red pepper, seeded and thinly
   sliced
1 medium cucumber, peeled and
   thinly sliced
2 tomatoes, thinly sliced
3 green onions with tops,
   chopped

6 black olives
2 tablespoons chopped fresh
   parsley
2 tablespoons chopped fresh mint
   leaves
   Parsley Dressing (see below)

Place the vegetables in a salad bowl. Add the olives and herbs. Pour in the dressing and mix lightly. Makes 6 servings, about 100 calories each.

Parsley Dressing: Mix together ¼ cup olive oil, 1 tablespoon vinegar, 1½ teaspoons lemon juice, salt and pepper to taste, and ⅓ cup chopped fresh parsley.

Pears and Kasseri

Core 6 pears with an apple or pear cutter and serve each one on a dessert plate with a square of cheese. Makes 6 servings, about 175 calories each.

$\mathcal{F}ar\text{-}\mathcal{E}astern$ $\mathcal{D}inner$ Serves 6

Curried Tomato Soup
Sesame Bean Sprout Salad
Five-Spice Roast Chicken
Squash with Green Onions
Gingered Papaya and Kiwi

Exotic Oriental seasonings—fresh and candied ginger, Chinese five-spice, and sesame seed—transform readily available ingredients into a Far Eastern repast. With the essentials at hand, this party or family meal goes together readily. The full spiciness in the soup comes from curry powder and fresh ginger root. (Ginger can be preserved for later use by tucking it in a bottle of sherry or vodka. It can also be frozen for shaving off a piece whenever needed.) Chinese five-spice is the seasoning that permeates the roast chicken. It is a combination of five seasonings, the most dominant being cinnamon, star anise, and cloves, and it is available in any Oriental market. A fast vegetable dish, a bean sprout salad, and fresh sliced tropical fruit complete this Oriental spread. For a wine, consider a Sylvaner or Chenin Blanc. The calorie count per person totals about 475 for this Oriental dinner.

Curried Tomato Soup

1 large onion, chopped
1 clove garlic, minced
1 teaspoon curry powder
1 teaspoon chopped fresh peeled ginger root
1 teaspoon butter
6 medium tomatoes, peeled, or 1 can (15 ounces) whole tomatoes

1 6-ounce can tomato paste
3 cups chicken broth (see page 26)
Salt
Freshly ground pepper
1 small avocado, peeled and diced

Using a large saucepot, sauté the onion, garlic, curry powder, and ginger in the butter until soft. Add the tomatoes, tomato paste, and chicken broth. Cover and simmer 30 minutes. Puree in batches in a blender or food processor. Season with salt and pepper to taste. ☆ Serve hot or cold, garnished with avocado. Makes 6 servings, about 75 calories each.

☆ Prepare 1 or 2 days in advance to this point.

Five-Spice Roast Chicken

1 broiler-fryer (3 pounds)*
½ teaspoon salt
¼ teaspoon freshly ground pepper
1 teaspoon Chinese five-spice
2 tablespoons soy sauce

2 tablespoons dry sherry
½ teaspoon chopped fresh peeled
 ginger root
1 clove garlic, minced
½ teaspoon sesame oil

Rub the bird with the salt, pepper and five-spice and place it on a rack in a baking pan. Roast in a 425° oven for 15 minutes. Mix together the soy, sherry, ginger, garlic, and sesame oil and brush part of this baste over the bird. Reduce heat to 375° and roast about 1 hour longer, basting with remaining sauce, until drumstick moves easily. ☆ Place on a platter for carving. Makes 4 to 6 servings, about 250 calories each.

☆ Prepare 1 day in advance to this point and serve cold, if desired.

* For heartier appetites roast 2 chickens.

Sesame Bean Sprout Salad

2 medium tomatoes, cut in
 wedges
1 cucumber, thinly sliced
4 cups bean sprouts
2 tablespoons salad oil
2 tablespoons lemon juice
2 tablespoons white wine vinegar
1 tablespoon soy sauce

½ teaspoon dry mustard
¼ teaspoon salt
 Generous dash of freshly
 ground pepper
 Salad greens
2 tablespoons toasted sesame
 seeds

Place the tomatoes, cucumber, and sprouts in a bowl. Mix together the oil, lemon juice, vinegar, soy, mustard, salt, and pepper. Pour this dressing over the vegetables and mix lightly. Spoon into 6 individual bowls lined with greens. Sprinkle with sesame seeds. Makes 6 servings, about 80 calories each.

Squash with Green Onions

6 small yellow crookneck squash
1 teaspoon salad oil
2 tablespoons chicken stock (see
    page 26)
2 green onions, chopped
¼ teaspoon salt
⅛ teaspoon freshly ground pepper

Trim the ends from squash and slice very thinly. Place the slices in a frying pan with the oil, stock, onions, and seasoning. Cover and steam for 3 to 4 minutes, or until crisp tender. Makes 6 servings, about 30 calories each.

Gingered Papaya and Kiwi

2 medium papaya
2 kiwi fruit
1 tablespoon finely chopped
    candied preserved ginger
1 lime, cut in wedges

Peel and slice papaya, discarding the seeds. Arrange on individual dessert plates. Peel and slice kiwi thinly and arrange alongside. Sprinkle with ginger and garnish with lime. Makes 6 servings, about 40 calories each.

French Country Dinner
Serves 6

Hearts of Palm Salad
Roast Chicken with Garlic
Herbed Green Beans
Raspberry Cheese Tart

A golden roasted bird and a pretty, open-face berry tart characterize French country dining at its best. The elements are transposed here for a festive yet easy to master summer dinner. The meal commences with a tantalizing hearts of palm salad. Garlic-scented chicken is paired with herb-basted green beans. For dessert, a round of pastry, swiftly made out of frozen puff pastry shells, is filled with brandied cheese and raspberries. A Chenin Blanc or White Burgundy suits this occasion. This French provincial dinner totals about 500 calories per person.

Hearts of Palm Salad

¼ cup olive oil
2 tablespoons white wine vinegar
2 teaspoons Dijon mustard
  Salt
½ teaspoon crumbled dried
    tarragon
1 can (11 ounces) hearts of palm
1 large head butter lettuce
2 tablespoons chopped fresh
    parsley
2 tablespoons chopped fresh
    chives
  Freshly ground pepper

For dressing, mix together the oil, vinegar, mustard, salt to taste, and the tarragon. Drain the palm hearts and slice them crosswise into ½-inch thick rounds. Tear greens into bite-sized pieces and place in a bowl. Pour the dressing over the greens and mix lightly. Add palm hearts and mix again. Sprinkle with parsley and chives. Makes 6 servings, about 100 calories each.

Roast Chicken with Garlic

1 broiler-fryer (3 pounds)*
Salt and pepper
1 tablespoon fresh tarragon or
rosemary, or ¾ teaspoon
crumbled dried tarragon
or rosemary

½ cup dry white vermouth
1 large head or bulb garlic
1 teaspoon butter

Season chicken with salt and pepper and sprinkle tarragon inside the cavity. Place on a rack in a roasting pan. Roast in a 425° oven for 20 minutes, then turn chicken to brown the bottom. Reduce heat to 375°, turn chicken upright, and cook 1 to 1¼ hours longer, basting with vermouth. The meat is ready when the drumstick moves easily. While the chicken is roasting, separate the garlic head into cloves, but do not peel the cloves. Simmer them in boiling water to cover for 5 minutes. Drain completely and repeat this process twice. Drain thoroughly. When cool enough to handle, slip the skins off the cloves. Sauté them in the butter for 2 to 3 minutes, or until lightly browned. Pour off the pan juices from the roasted chicken and skim the fat. Carve the meat and scatter several garlic cloves over each serving. Pass pan juices separately. Makes 4 to 6 servings, about 200 to 250 calories each.

* Roast 2 fryers, if desired.

Herbed Green Beans

1½ pounds green beans
Freshly ground pepper
1 tablespoon butter
1 tablespoon chopped fresh
parsley

1 tablespoon chopped fresh
chives
1 shallot, finely chopped
1 clove garlic, minced

Trim ends from beans and slice lengthwise. Cook them in boiling salted water until beans are crisp tender, about 5 to 7 minutes. Lift the cover occasionally to let the volatile acids escape. Drain well. Melt butter in a large frying pan. Add parsley, chives, shallot, garlic, and beans; shake pan to coat beans with the herbs. Makes 6 servings, about 50 calories each.

Raspberry Cheese Tart

2 frozen puff pastry shells, thawed (⅓ of a 10-ounce package) or homemade Quick Puff Pastry (see below)

3 ounces cream cheese

2 tablespoons plain yogurt

4 teaspoons brandy or cognac

2 tablespoons powdered sugar

½ teaspoon vanilla

1 pint raspberries, strawberries, or blueberries

2 tablespoons raspberry, red currant, or strawberry jelly, melted

Stack puff pastries on a floured board and roll them out with a rolling pin to form a 13- to 14-inch round. Place it on a pizza pan and freeze for 10 minutes to firm up dough solidly. Prick with a fork at 2-inch intervals. Bake in a 425° oven for 8 minutes, or until golden brown; let cool. ☆ Meanwhile, beat cheese, yogurt, brandy, sugar, and vanilla until blended. Spread this over the cooled pastry. Arrange berries on top. Drizzle with melted jelly and chill. Makes 8 servings, about 105 calories each.

☆ Prepare 1 day in advance to this point.

Quick Puff Pastry: In a large bowl, stir together 1½ cups all-purpose flour and ½ cup cake flour. Add 1½ cups (¾ pound) butter, cut into cubes, and mix with fingertips or a flat beater until butter is the size of large beans. Add ½ cup water and mix just until the dough clings together in a ball. Roll to a 12 by 12-inch rectangle and fold like a business letter. Make a one-quarter turn and repeat three more times. Refrigerate for 40 minutes and repeat the entire rolling process 2 more times, chilling between. At this point the pastry may be frozen. For ease later, cut it into 8 pieces, slip into a plastic bag, seal, and freeze. Makes about 24 ounces. Each one-eighth section of pastry is equivalent to 2 frozen puff pastry shells.

Portuguese Fish Cafe Dinner

Serves 4

Whole Steamed Artichokes
Fisherman's Seafood Platter
Pears and Brie

If you have access to fresh seafood, a platter of wine-steeped shellfish makes a splendid winter feast for guests. This entrée is the house specialty of a charming contemporary restaurant at the seaport resort of Cascais, Portugal. Each 2-foot-long serving dish comes heaped with several dozen tiny clams, coral mussels, succulent crayfish, and big shrimp with popping black eyes. A Continental dessert, such as fresh sliced pears and Brie cheese, is perfect. With a Portuguese Vinho Verde, a French Muscadet, or a California Johannisberg Riesling, the meal needs few accoutrements. The calorie count for this seafood feast is about 490 per person.

Whole Steamed Artichokes

- 4 large artichokes
- 2 cloves garlic, minced
- 1 tablespoon olive oil

Take off the outer leaves of the artichokes, cut off the stem end evenly, and trim the tips of the leaves with scissors. Place the artichokes in a steamer, drizzle with oil, and sprinkle the garlic on top. Steam over simmering water for 45 to 50 minutes, or just until tender. If desired, serve with a dish of hot mustard sauce, made by blending hot mustard with plain yogurt. Makes 4 servings, about 50 calories each.

Fisherman's Seafood Platter

2 dozen mussels or small rock
    clams
1 dozen large prawns
1 Dungeness crab, cracked, or
    2 lobster tails, split
¾ cup dry white vermouth
6 tablespoons chopped fresh
    cilantro or parsley
2 cloves garlic, minced
3 tablespoons butter
    Lemon wedges

Scrub shellfish thoroughly and place in a large soup kettle, along with the vermouth, 4 tablespoons of the cilantro, and the garlic. Cover and simmer for 5 to 10 minutes, or until the mussel or clam shells open. Transfer to a large platter and spoon the juices on top. Heat butter and the remaining 2 tablespoons cilantro until butter melts; spoon this over the shellfish. Garnish with lemon wedges. Accompany with dampened towels. Makes 4 servings, about 250 calories each.

Barbecue from Rhodes Serves 8

Spinach Salad with Sunflower Seeds
Butterflied Lamb
Asparagus with Kasseri
Melon Berry Bowl

Good cooks naturally pair many dishes. Spinach and lamb is one famous partnership. Here they mingle in a Greek barbecue meal, ideal for late spring and summer. Sunflower seeds and chopped egg spark a spinach salad that introduces the meal. Butterflied barbecued lamb offers an easy-to-carve entrée. Asparagus with crumbled Kasseri provides a fine balance. A melon and berry bowl, bathed in citrus juices, is the conclusion. Pour a Petite Sirah for a complementary accent. The calorie count is 450 per person for this barbecue dinner.

Spinach Salad with Sunflower Seeds

2	to 3 large bunches spinach
5	tablespoons olive oil
1½	tablespoons lemon juice
1½	tablespoons white wine vinegar
2	teaspoons Dijon mustard
½	teaspoon salt
	Generous dash of freshly ground pepper
2	tablespoons chopped fresh chives
2	hard-cooked eggs
2	tablespoons toasted sunflower seeds

Wash spinach well, pat dry, and tear into bite-sized pieces; chill. Mix together the oil, lemon juice, vinegar, mustard, salt, pepper, and chives. Place the spinach in a salad bowl, pour in the dressing, and mix lightly. Sieve the egg over all and sprinkle with sunflower seeds. Makes 8 servings, about 115 calories each.

Butterflied Lamb

1 small leg of lamb, boned and
      butterflied
1 cup dry red wine
3 tablespoons olive oil
4 cloves garlic, minced
1 sprig fresh rosemary, or
      1 teaspoon dried rosemary
1½ teaspoons salt
½ teaspoon freshly ground pepper
3 to 4 lemons, cut in half on a
      zig-zag

Have your butcher bone and butterfly the leg of lamb. Place the meat in a shallow dish. Mix together the wine, oil, garlic, rosemary, salt, and pepper and brush on the meat. Marinate, chilled, for several hours or overnight. Barbecue the lamb over medium coals, turning once, until medium-rare. Slice thinly. Garnish with lemon halves. Makes 8 servings, about 225 calories each.

Asparagus with Kasseri

2½ pounds fresh asparagus
3 tablespoons butter
⅓ cup freshly grated Kasseri or
      Romano cheese

Wash asparagus and cut off tough ends. Use a vegetable peeler to peel the lower part of the stalks. Cook in boiling salted water just until barely tender, about 7 minutes; drain. Turn onto a serving platter and keep warm. Heat the butter until it sizzles and starts to turn brown; pour it over the asparagus and sprinkle with cheese. Makes 8 servings, about 75 calories each.

Melon Berry Bowl

⅓ cup orange juice
3 tablespoons sugar
2 tablespoons lemon juice
2 tablespoons lime juice
   Grated peel of 1 orange
   Grated peel of 1 lemon
   Grated peel of 1 lime
2 cups watermelon balls
2 cups honeydew melon balls
1 cup raspberries
1 cup strawberries
   Mint sprigs

Combine orange juice and sugar in a saucepan and heat until sugar dissolves. Cool, then stir in the lemon juice, lime juice, citrus peels, melon balls and berries. Cover and chill at least 2 hours. Ladle into dessert bowls and garnish with mint. Makes 8 servings, about 40 calories each.

Cantonese Dinner   Serves 6

Smoked Oyster and Spinach Salad
Oriental Roast Chicken
Green Beans and Sprouts
Gingered Baked Papaya
Pineapple Ice

Oriental seasonings—soy, sesame seed, and ginger root—flavor this easy roast chicken dinner for all seasons. Smoked oysters lend a surprise to the first course, a spinach salad. The spicy roast chicken, good hot or cold, is served with a stir-fry of green beans and sprouts and a hot papaya boat. Dessert is a refreshing fruit ice, swiftly made in a food processor. A French Colombard or White Zinfandel would be in place here. The calorie count for this Oriental dinner is about 475 calories per person.

Smoked Oyster and Spinach Salad

1   bunch radishes, shredded
1   medium cucumber, shredded
6   tablespoons white vinegar
2   teaspoons sugar
1   teaspoon salt
1   can (4 ounces) smoked oysters, drained
1   pound spinach
2   tablespoons soy sauce
    Dash of sherry
2   tablespoons sesame seeds, toasted

Mix together the radishes, cucumber, 4 tablespoons of the vinegar, the sugar, and salt in a bowl and let stand 1 hour. Drain and place in the center of a platter. Top with the oysters. Parboil the spinach for 30 seconds in boiling salted water; drain and squeeze dry. Cut into 1-inch strips. Mix together the soy, the remaining 2 tablespoons vinegar, and the sherry in a bowl; add spinach and mix lightly. Ring the shredded vegetables with the spinach and sprinkle sesame seeds over the spinach. Makes 6 servings, about 55 calories each.

Oriental Roast Chicken

1   clove garlic, minced
1   shallot or green onion, minced
2   teaspoons finely chopped
      peeled fresh ginger root
¼   cup soy sauce
1   tablespoon dry sherry
1   teaspoon honey
1   broiler-fryer (3 pounds)*

Mix the garlic, shallots, and ginger with the soy, sherry, and honey. Add the chicken and let marinate, turning often, for 1 hour. Place on a rack in a broiling pan and roast in a 425° oven for 30 minutes. Reduce temperature to 350° and continue roasting 1 hour longer, basting occasionally with marinade, until chicken is tender and drumstick moves easily. Makes 4 to 6 servings, about 250 calories each.

* If desired roast 2 broiler-fryers, reserving leftovers.

Green Beans and Sprouts

1   pound green beans
1   medium onion, finely chopped
1   teaspoon olive oil
2   teaspoons soy sauce
1   pound bean sprouts

Trim ends from green beans and cut French-style. Cook in enough boiling salted water to cover until crisp tender, about 5 to 7 minutes; drain. Using a large frying pan or wok, sauté the onion in oil until tender and golden. Stir in the soy sauce and add the sprouts and green beans. Cook over high heat, stirring constantly, until hot. Makes 6 servings, about 50 calories each.

Gingered Baked Papaya

3 small papaya
1 tablespoon honey
2 tablespoons lime juice
2 teaspoons chopped peeled fresh
    ginger root
1 lime, cut in wedges

Cut papayas in half and scoop out seeds. Mix together the honey, lime juice, and ginger and spoon inside the half shells. Place on a baking pan and cover with foil. Bake in a 375° oven for 15 minutes or until hot. Garnish with lime. Makes 6 servings, about 60 calories each.

Pineapple Ice

1 medium pineapple
2 to 3 tablespoons sugar, or
    to taste

Halve the pineapple, core, and scoop out the fruit with a grapefruit knife. Cut fruit into 1-inch pieces. Purée in a food processor or blender, then force through a wire strainer; discard the stringy pulp. Sweeten the fruit purée with the sugar. Pour into a shallow baking pan and freeze until solid. Scoop into a food processor with the metal disc attached. Process until light and fluffy, like a thick slush. Return to the freezer until set. ☆ Spoon into dessert bowls and garnish with mint sprigs. Makes 6 servings, about 60 calories each.

☆ The ice may be made 2 to 3 weeks in advance to this point.

Normandy Fish Dinner *Serves 6*

Country-Style Hot Slaw
Snapper with Garlic Butter Sauce
Crookneck Squash with Basil
Peaches in Riesling

For an easy, swift dinner for unexpected guests, this Normandy poached fish menu fills the bill. It can go to the table in less than half an hour with the aid of a food processor or mechanical shredder to handle the slaw. A Pinot Blanc or good Chablis enhances this menu. The calorie count for this French dinner comes to about 390 per person.

Country-Style Hot Slaw

4   cups shredded cabbage
      (preferably part red)
2   carrots, peeled and shredded
2   green onions, finely chopped
6   tablespoons cider vinegar
¼   cup sugar
1   teaspoon dry mustard
1   teaspoon salt
      Generous dash of freshly
        ground pepper
2   tablespoons plain yogurt
2   tablespoons sour cream or
        crème fraîche (see page 57)

Place cabbage, carrots, and onions in a bowl. Place in a small saucepan the vinegar, sugar, mustard, salt, and pepper. Heat, stirring, until sugar melts and ingredients are well blended. Pour the hot dressing over the vegetables and mix well. Blend the yogurt and sour cream and stir into cabbage. Makes 6 servings, about 80 calories each.

Snapper with Garlic Butter Sauce

$1\frac{1}{2}$ pounds red snapper, sole, or
       turbot fillets
$\frac{1}{2}$ cup water
2 tablespoons lemon juice
2 tablespoons chopped shallots or
       green onions
$\frac{1}{2}$ teaspoon salt
$\frac{1}{2}$ teaspoon white pepper
$\frac{1}{3}$ cup dry white vermouth
$\frac{1}{3}$ cup white wine vinegar
2 cloves garlic, minced
3 tablespoons butter

Cut fish into serving-sized pieces. Place the water, lemon juice, shallots,
salt, and pepper in a large frying pan and bring to a boil. Then reduce
heat so that liquid just simmers. Add the fish and poach 5 to 6 minutes, or
until fish flakes with a fork. Meanwhile place vermouth, vinegar, and
garlic in a small saucepan. Bring to a boil and cook until reduced to $\frac{1}{4}$ cup
liquid. Add the butter 1 tablespoon at a time, beating it in until thick and
creamy. Remove from heat and season with more salt and white pepper to
taste. To serve, lift fish onto warmed plates and top with sauce. Makes 6
servings, about 165 calories each.

Crookneck Squash with Basil

1½ pounds small crookneck squash
Salt
2 teaspoons chopped fresh basil,
or ½ teaspoon crumbled
dried basil
1 clove garlic, minced
2 teaspoons butter
Generous dash of freshly
ground pepper

Trim the ends from squash and halve lengthwise. Cook, covered, in a small amount of boiling salted water until crisp tender, about 5 minutes; drain. Add basil, garlic, and butter and heat, shaking pan to coat. Sprinkle with pepper. Makes 6 servings, about 30 calories each.

Peaches in Riesling

6 peaches
1 bottle late harvest Johannisberg
Riesling or Champagne

Just before serving, peel and slice the peaches into large-bowled wine glasses. Pour the wine over them and serve. Makes 6 servings, about 115 calories each.

Dinner from Lyon Serves 6

Clam and Chicken Nectar
Capered Turbot in a Vegetable Cloak
Glazed Carrots
Lime Soufflé Léon de Lyon

The simple, sophisticated style of a French bistro characterizes this menu for all seasons. A warming broth is the starter. A quickly broiled fish, served with a mélange of colorful vegetables, is the entrée. Dessert is a light and lively lime soufflé, a specialty of a two-star restaurant in Lyon, the Léon de Lyon. The chef there occasionally substitutes lemon for the lime. Consider a dry Semillon or Riesling with the meal. The calorie count for this all-season dinner is about 430 per person.

Clam and Chicken Nectar

3 cups chicken stock (see
    page 26)
1½ cups clam or mussel broth or
    bottled clam juice
    Dash of celery salt
    Dash of liquid hot pepper
    seasoning
⅛ teaspoon salt
¼ cup heavy cream
    Chopped fresh chives or
    parsley

Combine the chicken and clam broths in a saucepan and add the celery salt and hot pepper seasoning. Bring to a boil, then reduce heat and simmer 10 minutes for flavors to blend. Meanwhile, add the salt to the cream and whip it until stiff. Ladle the broth into small bowls or cups and top with salted whipped cream. Sprinkle with chives. Makes 6 servings, about 40 calories each.

Capered Turbot in a Vegetable Cloak

1½ pounds turbot or sole fillets	3 medium tomatoes, peeled and diced
½ teaspoon salt	1 clove garlic, minced
Generous dash of freshly ground pepper	¼ cup chopped fresh parsley
1½ tablespoons lemon juice	1 tablespoon capers
6 teaspoons butter	1 tablespoon chopped fresh basil, or ¾ teaspoon crumbled dried basil
¾ pound mushrooms, thinly sliced	
1 bunch green onions, chopped	

Place fish fillets on a sheet of foil on a baking pan. Season with the salt and pepper and sprinkle with the lemon juice. Dot with 2 teaspoons of the butter. Using a large frying pan, sauté the mushrooms, onions, tomatoes, and garlic in the remaining 4 teaspoons butter for about 1 minute. Add the parsley, capers, and basil, stir, and remove from heat. Broil the fish until golden brown and completely cooked, about 4 minutes (it is not necessary to turn it). Transfer the fish to a platter or to individual plates and cover with the sautéed vegetables. Makes 6 servings, about 215 calories each.

Glazed Carrots

12 slender carrots
1 tablespoon butter
1 teaspoon sugar
1 tablespoon brandy or cognac
2 tablespoons chopped fresh parsley

Trim off the ends and peel the carrots. Cook in a small amount of boiling salted water until just tender, about 15 to 20 minutes; drain. Add to the pan the butter and sugar and heat, shaking the pan until the sugar caramelizes and the carrots are glazed. Add the brandy and reduce heat immediately, shaking the pan. Sprinkle with parsley. Makes 6 servings, about 55 calories each.

Lime Soufflé Léon de Lyon

Juice and freshly grated peel of
2 limes
6 **tablespoons granulated sugar**
4 **egg whites**
4 **eggs, separated**
⅛ **teaspoon salt**
⅛ **teaspoon cream of tartar**
2 **teaspoons powdered sugar**

Place lime peel in a small bowl, add 1 teaspoon of the granulated sugar and mash with the back of a spoon to extract the oils. Beat the 8 egg whites until foamy; add the salt and cream of tartar, and whip until soft peaks form. Beat in 2 tablespoons of the granulated sugar and whip until stiff. In another bowl, beat the egg yolks until pale and lemon colored, then add the remaining granulated sugar, the lime juice, and the peel, beating well. Fold one-third of the whites into the yolks, then fold in the remaining whites. Turn into a buttered 10½-inch round baking dish or a 1½-quart souffle dish with a collar. ☆ Dust the top with powdered sugar shaken through a wire strainer. Bake in a 400° oven for 12 to 15 minutes, or until set and the top is golden brown. Makes 6 servings, about 120 calories each.

☆ Prepare up to 1 hour in advance to this point. Let stand in dish at room temperature.

Pacific Barbecue Serves 8

Tomato Citrus Broth
Far Eastern London Broil
Mixed Vegetable Stir Fry
Gingered Melon Balls

An easy barbecue dinner is a splendid way to celebrate Indian summer with friends, and a marinated and grilled London broil makes a spectacular entrée. It's also neat to handle for a group. Here flavors of the Pacific—soy and sesame—permeate the meat. A fresh vegetable stir-fry makes a fine accompaniment. Consider offering jicama or halved white mushrooms sprinkled with lime juice and chile powder for an appetizer. Then pass the tomato citrus broth before the entrée. At the end of the meal, gingered melon balls refresh the palate. Pour a Cabernet Sauvignon to provide an elegant balance. The total calorie count for this barbecue dinner is only 325 per person.

Tomato Citrus Broth

2 cups beef consommé	⅓ cup lime or lemon juice
2 cups tomato juice	½ teaspoon celery salt
1 cup orange juice	Chopped fresh chives

Combine the consommé and juices. Season with celery salt. Serve hot or cold garnished with chives. Makes 8 servings, about 25 calories each.

Far Eastern London Broil

2 tablespoons soy sauce	2 cloves garlic, minced
2 tablespoons red wine	1 London broil (top
½ teaspoon sesame oil	round steak, 2 pounds)

Mix together the soy, wine, oil, and garlic in a shallow baking pan. Place the meat in this marinade and let stand 1 hour, basting occasionally. Broil or barbecue over low coals. Makes 8 servings, about 225 calories each.

Mixed Vegetable Stir-Fry

2 small zucchini, sliced in rounds
2 yellow crookneck squash, sliced
3 green onions, chopped
3 tablespoons chicken stock (see page 26)
2 stalks celery, sliced on the diagonal

$1\frac{1}{2}$ cups bean sprouts
1 clove garlic, minced
2 tablespoons soy sauce
2 tomatoes, cut in wedges
Salt
Freshly ground pepper

Heat a large frying pan or wok to a moderately high heat. Add the zucchini, crookneck squash, onions, and chicken stock and cook, stirring, for 2 minutes. Add the celery, bean sprouts, garlic, and soy sauce and cook 1 minute longer, or until vegetables are crisp tender. Add the tomatoes and season with salt and pepper to taste just before serving. Makes 8 servings, about 25 calories each.

Gingered Melon Balls

3 cups honeydew melon balls
3 cups watermelon balls
1 tablespoon lime juice
$\frac{1}{4}$ cup orange juice
$\frac{1}{2}$ teaspoon freshly grated lime peel

$\frac{1}{2}$ teaspoon freshly grated orange peel
1 tablespoon honey
1 tablespoon thinly sliced peeled fresh ginger root

Place the melon balls in a bowl. Stir together the citrus juices, peels, honey, and ginger root and spoon over the melon balls, mixing lightly. Cover and chill 1 hour before serving. Makes 8 servings, about 50 calories each.

Spanish Party Dinner Serves 6

Green Peppercorn Tomato Sorbet
Turbot Barcelona
Zucchini Fans
Orange Soufflé Séville

Tomatoes, oranges, lemons, olives, mint, and seafood punctuate Spanish cuisine, offering zest and lively colors. These elements keynote this refreshing summer party meal. It can be accomplished swiftly—most of it can be done at the last minute in about half an hour. As a starter, green peppercorns enliven a frosty tomato-mint sherbet. The vegetable ice is a breeze to make using a food processor. It is best served while still slushy, like a snow cone, rather than frozen solid. For the entrée, a coterie of vegetables blanket a turbot fillet during oven baking. Zucchini cut in a fan-shaped design provide a decorative vegetable accent. The assertive orange soufflé, made with undiluted orange juice concentrate, provides intense flavor in a lean manner. For wine, serve a Fumé Blanc, if you like. The calorie count totals 440 per person for this Latin menu.

Green Peppercorn Tomato Sorbet

6   large tomatoes, peeled, or 1 can
    (15 ounces) whole tomatoes
1   tablespoon lemon juice
1   tablespoon red wine vinegar
2   teaspoons green peppercorns,
    rinsed and drained

1   clove garlic, minced
1   green onion, chopped
1½   teaspoons salt
¼   teaspoon freshly ground pepper
1   tablespoon chopped fresh mint
    Mint sprigs or watercress

In a blender or food processor fitted with a steel blade, purée the tomatoes, lemon juice, vinegar, peppercorns, garlic, onion, salt, pepper, and chopped mint until smoothly blended. Pour into a shallow pan and freeze until just solid. Spoon half the mixture into a food processor (again with steel blade attached) or an electric mixer and beat until slushy. Add the remaining mixture and continue to process until slushy and lightly whipped. Turn into a refrigerator container, cover, and freeze until set. ☆ To serve, spoon into small bowls or large wine glasses and garnish with mint sprigs. Makes 6 servings, about 35 calories each.

☆ Prepare 2 weeks in advance to this point.

Turbot Barcelona

1   bunch green onions, chopped
1   teaspoon olive oil
3   medium carrots, peeled and
    grated
1   clove garlic, minced
1   strip (½ by 2½ inches) lemon
    peel, sliced into julienne
    strips
1   strip (½ by 2½ inches) orange
    peel, sliced into julienne strips
    Dash of mace or nutmeg
½   teaspoon salt
    Generous dash of freshly
    ground pepper
1½ pounds turbot or sole fillets
6   pimiento-stuffed olives, sliced
¼   cup dry white wine or vermouth

Using a large frying pan, sauté the onions in oil until glazed. Add the carrots and garlic and sauté 1 minute. Mix in the citrus peels, mace, salt, and pepper. Remove from heat. Place fish fillets in a greased shallow baking dish and season with more salt and pepper. Cover with a blanket of the vegetables and scatter olives over the top. Pour in the wine. Lay a sheet of foil loosely on top. Bake in a 375° oven for 15 to 20 minutes, or until fish flakes with a fork. Makes 6 servings, about 240 calories each.

Zucchini Fans

6   small to medium zucchini
1½ teaspoons olive oil
1   clove garlic, minced
2   teaspoons fresh chopped basil,
    or ½ teaspoon crumbled
    dried basil

Trim the ends from zucchini and slice lengthwise, at ¼-inch intervals, to a point about 1 inch from the other end. Cook in boiling salted water until crisp tender, about 5 to 7 minutes. Drain well and return to pan. Add the oil, garlic, and basil to the pan and heat, shaking vegetables until lightly coated. Makes 6 servings, about 35 calories each.

Orange Soufflé Séville

1 teaspoon freshly grated lemon
   peel
4 tablespoons sugar
4 eggs, separated
4 egg whites
⅛ teaspoon salt
⅛ teaspoon cream of tartar
5 tablespoons undiluted orange
   juice concentrate
1½ cups strawberries, whole with
   stems or sliced

In a small bowl mash the lemon peel with ½ teaspoon of the sugar. In another bowl, whip all 8 egg whites until foamy. Add the salt and cream of tartar and whip until soft peaks form, then beat in 2 tablespoons of the sugar and set aside. With the same beater, whip the egg yolks and remaining sugar until thick and lemon colored. Beat in the orange concentrate. Fold one-third of the egg whites into the yolk mixture to lighten them. Then fold the yolk mixture into all the whites. Turn into a buttered 1½-quart soufflé dish with a foil collar attached or into a 10½-inch round baking dish. ☆ Bake in a 375° oven for 20 to 25 minutes, or until golden brown and set. Serve at once. Pass berries separately. Makes 6 servings, about 130 calories each.

☆ Prepare up to 1 hour in advance to this point. Let batter stand at room temperature.

Dad's Splendid Dinner Serves 6

Spinach with Snow Mushrooms
Flank Steak Flambé
Carrot and Apple Whip
Broccoli Purée
Amaretto Chocolate Mousse

With the trend to "men in the kitchen" on the upswing, this elegant dinner will appeal to a man's culinary prowess and style. It is easy enough for a novice and utilizes the latest equipment. Diminutive mushrooms top a spinach salad, the steak is flamed, and the chocolate mousse has a lovely almond scent. This is a splendid feast to partner with a Cabernet Sauvignon or St. Emilion. The calorie count for this menu totals about 570 per person.

Spinach with Snow Mushrooms

2   bunches spinach
4   ounces alfalfa sprouts
1   cup halved cherry tomatoes
     (about 15)
     Spicy Dressing (see below)
4   ounces enoki (snow)
     mushrooms* or regular
     mushrooms, sliced
2   tablespoons toasted salted
     sunflower seeds

Tear spinach into bite-sized pieces, discarding stems, and place in a salad bowl. Add the sprouts and tomatoes. Chill until serving time. To serve, pour in the dressing and scatter the tiny mushrooms and sunflower seeds on top. Makes 6 servings, about 110 calories each.

Spicy Dressing: Combine 3 tablespoons white wine vinegar, 1 tablespoon dry white wine, 1½ teaspoons soy sauce, ¾ teaspoon salt, ¾ teaspoon dry mustard, ¾ teaspoon curry powder, ½ teaspoon sugar, and ¼ teaspoon freshly ground pepper, stirring until dissolved. Mix in ⅓ cup safflower oil. Shake well and chill.

* Enoki mushrooms are miniature mushrooms newly available in many good produce markets.

Flank Steak Flambé

1	flank steak (1 ½ pounds)	6	tablespoons dry red wine
	Salt	6	tablespoons beef stock
	Freshly ground pepper		(see page 38)
2	tablespoons butter	1	teaspoon Dijon mustard
2	tablespoons brandy or cognac	1	tablespoon chopped fresh parsley
2	shallots or green onions, chopped	1	tablespoon chopped fresh chives
1	clove garlic, minced		

Season meat with salt and pepper to taste.

Using a large frying pan, sauté meat in 1 tablespoon of the butter, turning to brown both sides and cooking until barely medium rare. Ignite the brandy and pour it, flaming, over the meat. Remove to a carving board. Add the shallots, garlic, wine, stock, and mustard to the pan and cook down juices until reduced by half. Add remaining 1 tablespoon butter, swirling it in. Slice the meat thinly on the diagonal and spoon the sauce over the slices. Sprinkle with parsley and chives. Makes 6 servings, about 230 calories each.

Carrot and Apple Whip

4	large carrots, peeled and sliced	¼	teaspoon freshly ground pepper
1	Golden Delicious or tart cooking apple, peeled and sliced	2	teaspoons butter
½	cup water	2	tablespoons chopped parsley or chives
½	teaspoon salt		

Place the carrot and apple slices in a pan with the water, salt, and pepper and simmer until tender, reserving liquid. Puree in a food processor with the butter, adding more water, if necessary, to make a light whip. Turn into a bowl and keep warm. Sprinkle with parsley or chives. Makes 6 servings, about 40 calories each.

Broccoli Purée

1 large bunch broccoli
2 teaspoons butter
  Freshly ground nutmeg

Cut broccoli into flowerets and peel the stems, then slice them. Cook in boiling salted water until tender; drain, reserving liquid. Purée the broccoli in a food processor with ⅓ cup cooking liquid, the butter, and nutmeg to taste, processing until light and fluffy. Turn into a bowl and keep warm. Makes 6 servings, about 30 calories each.

Amaretto Chocolate Mousse

⅔ cup semisweet chocolate bits
  (4 ounces)
2 tablespoons strong coffee
2 tablespoons Amaretto liqueur
1 teaspoon vanilla
4 eggs, separated
1 tablespoon sugar
2 tablespoons toasted slivered
  almonds

Place the chocolate bits and coffee in a metal bowl and heat in a 300° oven for 10 minutes, or until melted (do not overheat). (Or melt in a small pan placed over simmering—not boiling—water.) Remove from oven and stir in liqueur. Mix in the egg yolks, one at a time. Stir in the vanilla. Beat the egg whites until soft peaks form, then add the sugar, beating until stiff. Stir one-third of the whites into the chocolate mixture, then fold in the remaining whites. Turn into 6 dessert bowls, parfait glasses, or wine glasses. Cover and chill until set, about 2 hours. Sprinkle with toasted almonds at serving time. Makes 6 servings, about 160 calories each.

Make-Ahead Dinners

Moroccan Dinner • Indian Barbecue • Mexican
Holiday Buffet • Greek Country Dinner •
Florentine Family Dinner • Summer Dinner
from the Côte D'Azur • Summer
Smörgasbord • Trattoria Dinner from
Bologna • Djakarta Dinner

Moroccan Dinner Serves 6

Spicy Carrot Soup
Veal and Mangos Marrekesh
Sugar Pea and Mushroom Salad
Crème de Menthe Ice in Lime Shells

The scintillating spices of the Moroccan kitchen—cumin, allspice, and ginger root—accented with honey and lime juice make this dinner aromatic and attractive. A smooth carrot soup is the starter. The stellar entrée is a meal by itself. Sweet-and-sour veal chops are garnished with brilliant orange mango slices, green pistachios, and lime wedges. Follow with a crunchy sugar pea salad and finish with a refreshing mint ice. This is the setting for a Pinot Noir Blanc. This special dinner totals about 485 calories per person.

Spicy Carrot Soup

- 6 medium carrots, peeled
- 1 medium onion, quartered
- 2 cloves garlic, peeled
- 3 cups chicken stock
  (see page 26)
- 1 teaspoon cumin
- 1 teaspoon allspice
- ½ teaspoon salt
- ¼ teaspoon freshly ground pepper
  Dash of liquid hot pepper
  seasoning
- 1 tablespoon chopped fresh
  cilantro or parsley

Using a large saucepan, simmer the carrots, onion, and garlic in the chicken stock with the cumin, allspice, salt, and pepper until all vegetables are tender, about 12 to 15 minutes. Purée in a blender or food processor. Add the hot pepper seasoning. Ladle into bowls and sprinkle with cilantro. Makes 6 servings, about 40 calories each.

Veal and Mangos Marrekesh

1 large onion, chopped
2 teaspoons chopped peeled
    fresh ginger root
1 teaspoon cumin
½ teaspoon allspice
1 small stick cinnamon
2 cloves garlic, minced
½ teaspoon butter
6 veal chops
1 tablespoon honey
1½ tablespoons lime juice
1 mango
2 tablespoons chopped pistachios
1 lime, cut in wedges

Using a large frying pan with a lid, sauté the onion, ginger, cumin, all-spice, cinnamon, and garlic in butter for 2 to 3 minutes, or until onion is well coated. Add the veal chops and brown lightly on both sides. Cover and cook on low heat for 30 to 40 minutes, or until tender. Remove chops and keep warm. Add the honey and lime juice to the pan drippings and bring to a boil, stirring. Place a chop on each plate and spoon some sauce on top. Peel and slice the mango and arrange 2 slices on each chop. Sprinkle with nuts and garnish with lime wedges, to be squeezed over the chops. Makes 6 servings, about 260 calories each.

Sugar Pea and Mushroom Salad

⅓ cup olive oil
2 tablespoons lemon juice
2 tablespoons red wine vinegar
1 tablespoon Dijon mustard
½ teaspoon salt
 Generous dash of freshly ground pepper
½ pound mushrooms, thinly sliced

¼ pound sugar peas, ends trimmed
2 green onions, chopped
1 bunch radishes, sliced
1 head butter lettuce, torn into bite-sized pieces
 A few leaves endive or chicory

For dressing, mix together well the oil, lemon juice, vinegar, mustard, salt, and pepper; chill. Place mushrooms in a large salad bowl, pour on half of the dressing and mix lightly. Add sugar peas, onions, radishes, lettuce, and endive. Add the remaining dressing and mix lightly. Makes 6 servings, about 100 calories each.

Crème de Menthe Ice in Lime Shells

6 limes
1½ pints crème de menthe, lemon, or lime sherbet
2 tablespoons green crème de menthe
 Blossoms

Cut the tops off the limes about one-third of the way down and ream the fruit, saving the juice for another purpose. Fill the lime shells with sherbet, rounding the tops, and freeze until firm. ☆ To serve, place crushed ice in dessert bowls and nestle the filled lime shells in the center. Drizzle the liqueur over the shells and garnish each with a fuschia, daisy, or violet. Makes 6 servings, about 85 calories each.

☆ Prepare up to 2 weeks in advance to this point.

Indian Barbecue   Serves 6

Cumin Cucumber Salad
Chicken Tandoori
Green Beans with Jicama
Kiwi Medley with Lime

In the Indian style, deftly seasoned fruits and vegetables accompany a classic barbecued chicken. An Indian friend shared his way of toasting the spices for the chicken that turns out an outstanding version of the dish. A cumin-spiced salad, accented with beans, jicama, and colorful fresh fruits, is the balance of the spread. Consider a Sylvaner or White Zinfandel for sipping. The calorie count for this Indian barbecue is about 335 per person.

Cumin Cucumber Salad

1	teaspoon cumin seeds
1	cup small-curd cottage cheese
1	cup yogurt
	Salt
	Freshly ground pepper
2	medium cucumbers, peeled, seeded, and diced
1	bunch green onions, chopped
3	tomatoes, peeled and coarsely chopped
3	tablespoons chopped fresh parsley
	Romaine leaves

Toast the cumin seeds in a dry pan over medium heat for about 1 minute, shaking the pan so the seeds do not brown. Combine them with the cottage cheese, yogurt, and salt and pepper to taste, mixing well. Place the cucumber, onions, tomatoes, and parsley in a bowl. Add the dressing, mix lightly, and refrigerate 1 hour. Spoon into Romaine leaves to serve. Makes 6 servings, about 55 calories each.

Chicken Tandoori

$\frac{1}{4}$ teaspoon saffron threads
$1\frac{1}{2}$ tablespoons coriander seeds
1 teaspoon cumin seeds
3 whole cloves
   Seeds of 4 cardamom pods
1 hot red pepper
$\frac{3}{4}$ cup plain yogurt
$\frac{1}{2}$ medium onion, quartered
1 tablespoon chopped peeled
      fresh ginger root
1 large clove garlic, peeled
1 broiler-fryer ($3\frac{1}{2}$ pounds), or 6
      split chicken breasts, cut in
      pieces and skinned
1 lemon, cut in wedges

Soak the saffron in 2 tablespoons boiling water a few minutes. Meanwhile, using a heavy frying pan, roast the coriander and cumin seeds, cloves, cardamom, and pepper for 10 to 15 minutes over low heat, stirring or shaking the pan frequently. Place the yogurt, onion, ginger, and garlic in a blender or food processor and blend until smooth. Add the roasted seeds and the soaked saffron and its liquid and blend smooth. Place the chicken pieces in a bowl and pour in the marinade. Marinate in the refrigerator at least 2 hours or overnight. Broil or barbecue over medium coals, turning to brown both sides. Garnish with lemon wedges. Makes 4 to 6 servings, about 200 calories each.

Green Beans with Jicama

2 pounds green beans
1 tablespoon butter
1 small jicama, peeled and sliced
      (about ½ cup), or 1 can
      (4 ounces) water chestnuts,
      drained and thinly sliced
2 green onions, chopped
1 tablespoon chopped fresh
      parsley
   Salt
   Freshly ground pepper

Trim the ends from green beans and cut them in julienne strips. Cook in a large pot of boiling salted water until crisp tender; drain. Melt the butter in a frying pan; add the beans, jicama, onions, parsley, and salt and pepper to taste and heat, shaking pan, until the vegetables are heated. Makes 6 servings, about 40 calories each.

Kiwi Medley with Lime

3 kiwi
1 large or 2 small mangos
1 cup blueberries, raspberries, or
      seedless grapes
1 lime, cut in wedges

Peel and thinly slice the kiwi and arrange in dessert bowls. Peel and dice the mangos and scatter them over the kiwi. Sprinkle the berries or grapes on top. Garnish with a lime wedge. Makes 6 servings, about 40 calories each.

$\mathcal{M}$exican $\mathcal{H}$oliday $\mathcal{B}$uffet Serves 8

Smoky Barbecued Turkey
Mexican Salsa
Red Pepper Jelly
Colache
Orange, Cucumber, and Jicama Salad
Spiced Kahlua Ice

For a holiday buffet, this Mexican menu lends itself beautifully to enter-
taining a crowd, since the recipes may be doubled with ease. The turkey
develops a subtle smoky flavor during barbecuing that intensifies nicely
upon chilling. Two sauces—salsa and red pepper jelly—accompany it, as
do a hot, colorful corn and squash casserole and a crunchy jicama-
sparked orange salad. Dessert is a Kahlua-punctuated ice that belies its
slim calorie count. Serve a Gamay Rosé or a Gamay Beaujolais with this
festive meal. This menu averages about 445 calories per person.

Smoky Barbecued Turkey

1 turkey (8 to 12 pounds)	3 cloves garlic, finely chopped
Salt	1 lemon, sliced
Freshly ground pepper	

Season turkey with salt and pepper. Tuck garlic and lemon inside the
larger cavity. Place on a barbecue grill, cover, and cook over medium-low
(about 325°) coals until a meat thermometer inserted in the thickest part
of the thigh registers 175°. Remove to a platter. Serve hot or chilled. (The
smoky flavor intensifies upon chilling.) Makes 8 to 10 servings, and each
has about 200 calories.

Mexican Salsa

4 tomatoes, peeled and diced	2 tablespoons canned green chile
3 green onions, chopped	peppers
¼ cup chopped fresh	1 teaspoon salt
parsley	Generous dash of freshly
3 tablespoons chopped fresh	ground pepper
cilantro	¼ teaspoon dried oregano
1 clove garlic, minced	

Combine all ingredients in a large bowl and mix well. Cover and chill
several hours. Makes about 2½ cups, at 4 calories per tablespoon.

Red Pepper Jelly

6 large red peppers, halved and seeded	1½ cups white or cider vinegar
2 tablespoons salt	6 cups sugar
	1 bottle (7 ounces) pectin

Finely chop the peppers, by hand or in a food processor. Turn into a large baking pan, sprinkle with the salt, and let stand 30 minutes. Drain and rinse under cold water. Place the peppers in a kettle and add the vinegar and sugar. Bring to a boil and add the pectin. Boil until jelly is thick and "sheets" when dropped from a spoon, about 20 minutes. Pour into hot sterilized jars and seal immediately. Makes about 2 pints, at 55 calories per tablespoon.

Colache

1 teaspoon butter	½ teaspoon salt
1 medium onion, finely chopped	⅛ teaspoon freshly ground pepper
3 medium zucchini, sliced	2 ears corn, cut from cob, or 1½ cups frozen corn, thawed
3 medium crookneck squash, sliced	2 medium tomatoes, peeled and diced
1 red or green pepper, diced	
⅓ cup water	

In a large frying pan, melt the butter and add onion, zucchini, crookneck squash, and pepper. Sauté for a few minutes, stirring. Mix in the water, salt, and pepper and simmer for 5 minutes. Add the corn and tomatoes and cook for 3 minutes longer, or until vegetables are crisp tender. Makes 8 servings, about 55 calories each.

Orange, Cucumber, and Jicama Salad

1 large head Romaine	1 small red pepper, diced
2 navel oranges, peeled and thinly sliced	⅓ cup olive or salad oil
1 cucumber, peeled and sliced	3 tablespoons white wine vinegar
1 small sweet red onion, sliced into rings	½ teaspoon salt
¾ cup chopped peeled jicama	½ teaspoon crumbled oregano
	Generous dash of freshly ground pepper

Tear Romaine into bite-sized pieces and place in a salad bowl. Arrange the oranges, cucumber, onion, jicama, and pepper on top. Mix together well the oil, vinegar, salt, oregano and pepper. Pour this dressing over the salad and mix lightly. Makes 8 servings, about 90 calories each.

Spiced Kahlua Ice

¼ cup brown sugar
2 cups water
3½ teaspoons freeze-dried coffee
1 stick cinnamon
6 whole cloves
¼ cup coffee liqueur, such as Kahlua
½ teaspoon vanilla

Combine the sugar, water, coffee, cinnamon, and cloves in a saucepan. Bring just to boiling, then remove from heat and let cool. Pour through a strainer to remove whole spices and stir in the liqueur and vanilla. Pour into a shallow 9-inch pan and freeze until solid. Transfer to a food processor or electric mixer and process until light and fluffy. Return to the freezer and freeze until solid. ☆ Makes 6 servings, about 45 calories each.

☆ Prepare up to 2 weeks in advance to this point.

Greek Country Dinner　Serves 6

Aegean Salad
Lamb and Pine Nut Pitas
Vegetable Skewers
Summer Beans with Garlic
Nectarines with Honey Lime Cream

Greek peasant fare is perfect for the slim regime. The abundant use of fresh vegetables and fruits is only one of its many assets. Toning down the traditional olive oil is the secret to the lower calories here. Filo dough provides a crisp shell for a lamb, pine nut, and Parmesan filling, which is a tantalizing make-ahead entrée. The dough is available in Mediterranean specialty food shops and some delicatessens. A country salad, fresh green beans, a skewer of fresh and marinated vegetables, and seasonal fruit complete the spread. A Ruby Cabernet or Gamay belongs in this company. This Greek dinner has about 550 calories per person.

Aegean Salad

1　tablespoon olive oil
3　tablespoons red wine vinegar
1　tablespoon Dijon mustard
$\frac{1}{2}$　teaspoon salt
　　Generous dash of freshly ground pepper
$\frac{1}{2}$　teaspoon crumbled dried oregano
2　cucumbers, peeled and sliced or diced

4　tomatoes, sliced or cut into wedges
3　green onions, chopped
1　tablespoon chopped fresh parsley
1　ounce feta cheese
$1\frac{1}{2}$　dozen Mediterranean olives

For the dressing, mix together well the oil, vinegar, mustard, salt, pepper, and oregano. Place the cucumbers, tomatoes, onions, and parsley in a large bowl. Add the dressing and mix lightly. Spoon into individual bowls and garnish with crumbled cheese and olives. Makes 6 servings, about 80 calories each.

Lamb and Pine Nut Pitas

1	large onion, chopped	½	cup freshly grated Parmesan cheese
3	tablespoons butter		
⅓	pound mushrooms, sliced	2	egg whites
1	pound ground lamb	2	tablespoons pine nuts
1	teaspoon salt	2	tablespoons chopped fresh parsley
½	teaspoon allspice		
1	clove garlic, minced	6	sheets filo dough

Using a large frying pan, sauté the onion in 1 teaspoon of the butter until golden. Add 1 more teaspoon butter and the mushrooms and cook until glazed. Remove to a large bowl. Place the lamb, salt, allspice, and garlic in the frying pan and cook until meat is browned. Add this mixture to the mushrooms and mix in the cheese, egg whites, pine nuts (pistachios are also good), and parsley. Lay out 1 filo sheet. Melt the remaining butter and brush some of it lightly over half the sheet. Fold the sheet in half and brush with butter again. Place a spoonful of filling along the edge of a short side, staying 1 inch from the longer sides, and fold that 1-inch piece over the filling. Roll up the short side and place seam side down on a greased baking sheet. Repeat until all the filo sheets and filling are used, and place the rolls 1 inch apart on a baking sheet. Brush their tops with melted butter. ☆ Bake in a 375° oven for 15 to 20 minutes, or until golden. Makes 6 servings, about 300 calories each.

☆ Prepare in advance to this point and freeze the rolls, covered. Let thaw before baking.

Vegetable Skewers

6	stuffed grape leaves (see page 165, or buy them canned)
6	mushroom caps
6	cherry tomatoes
6	marinated artichoke hearts

Alternate the vegetables on 6 skewers; chill. (Note: Easier to do this ahead of time.) Serve with the lamb pitas. Makes 6 servings, about 30 calories each.

Summer Beans with Garlic

1½ pounds Italian or regular green
    beans
1 tablespoon olive oil
2 cloves garlic, minced

1 green onion, chopped
2 tablespoons minced fresh
    parsley

Trim the ends from beans and cut in ½-inch lengths. Cook in a large amount of boiling salted water until crisp tender, about 7 minutes; drain. Heat the oil in a large frying pan; add the garlic and onion and cook 1 minute. Add the beans and shake the pan until they are coated with seasonings. Sprinkle with parsley. Makes 6 servings, about 40 calories each.

Nectarines with Honey Lime Cream

½ cup plain yogurt
¼ cup sour cream
1 tablespoon lime juice
1 tablespoon honey

1 teaspoon freshly grated lime
    peel
    Dash of mace or cardamom
6 nectarines

Mix together the yogurt, sour cream, lime juice, honey, lime peel, and mace. Cover and refrigerate until serving time. Peel and slice nectarines into large-bowled wine glasses or dessert bowls and spoon the honey cream on top. Makes 8 servings, about 100 calories each.

Florentine Family Dinner *Serves 8*

Sorrel Soup
Stuffed Veal Camillo
Green Beans with Herbs
Cherry Tomato and Olive Salad
Galliano Zabaglione with Peaches

Patterned after a Florentine family-style trattoria dinner, this is a splendid meal for summer. Since several dishes can be served hot or cold, it lends itself to either a gala course-by-course banquet or a midday picnic. The starting point is an aromatic sorrel soup. Sorrel is a bit elusive in the marketplace, but it can be found. You may wish to plant your own. A succulent veal roll studded with pistachios and shredded carrot is superb hot or cold. Joining it are a cherry tomato salad and herb-strewn green beans. Sliced peaches in a Galliano-scented zabaglione are the finale. As an alternative dessert for a picnic outing, serve the peaches sans sauce, but with a splash of Galliano added on the spot. Consider a Gewürztraminer or Grenache Rosé for sipping. This midsummer meal has about 515 calories per person.

Sorrel Soup

5 green onions, chopped (white part only)	4 cups chicken stock (see page 26)
½ teaspoon butter	4 teaspoons cornstarch
1 cup chopped sorrel leaves	2 tablespoons cold water
	2 egg yolks

Using a large saucepot, sauté the onions in butter until glazed. Add the sorrel and cook over low heat until it changes from a bright green to a muddy color. Add the chicken stock and bring to a boil. Mix together the cornstarch and cold water; stir in this paste and cook until the broth is thickened. Purée in a blender or food processor. Add the yolks and purée smooth. Reheat just until hot, without boiling. Makes 8 servings, about 30 calories each.

Stuffed Veal Camillo

1 breast of veal (2 pounds), with bones	¼ teaspoon nutmeg
3 cups water	1 teaspoon salt
3 chicken bouillon cubes	⅛ teaspoon freshly ground pepper
1 carrot, peeled	3 tablespoons nonfat dry milk
1 large onion	3 tablespoons chopped fresh parsley
½ teaspoon olive oil	1 clove garlic, minced
½ pound lean ground veal	1 teaspoon freshly grated lemon peel
½ pound lean ground pork	½ teaspoon crumbled dried tarragon
1 slice brioche or good white bread, crumbled	12 shelled pistachios
1 egg white	
1 egg	

Remove bones from the veal, leaving a large solid piece of meat, and brown the bones lightly in a heavy, dry Dutch oven. Add the water and bouillon cubes and simmer 30 minutes; remove the bones. Shred the carrot and onion (using a food processor, if desired) and, in a frying pan, sauté in oil until soft. In a large bowl, mix together the ground meats, brioche, egg white, egg, nutmeg, salt, pepper, powdered milk, parsley, garlic, lemon peel, and tarragon. Lightly pound the veal breast to an even thickness, using a cleaver. Spread it with the ground meat mixture and sprinkle with pistachios. Roll up from the narrow end and tie with string in several places. Wrap it in cheesecloth and poach in the chicken broth for 2 hours, or until tender. ☆ Serve hot or chilled. Makes 8 servings, about 275 calories each.

☆ The roll may be prepared 2 to 3 days in advance.

Green Beans with Herbs

2 pounds green beans
2 shallots or green onions, chopped
½ teaspoon olive oil
1 clove garlic, minced
2 teaspoons fresh chopped tarragon, or ½ teaspoon crumbled dried tarragon
2 tablespoons minced fresh parsley

Trim ends from the beans and slice lengthwise (French-cut). Cook the beans in boiling salted water until crisp tender, about 7 to 10 minutes; drain. While the beans are cooking, sauté the shallots in oil with the garlic until soft. Add the beans, tarragon, and parsley and shake the pan to coat. Makes 8 servings, about 20 calories each.

Cherry Tomato and Olive Salad

2 pounds cherry tomatoes
3 tablespoons olive oil
1 tablespoon brandy or cognac
½ teaspoon salt
   Generous dash of freshly ground pepper
   Butter lettuce
¼ cup Mediterranean olives
3 tablespoons chopped fresh basil, chives, and parsley, mixed together

Halve the tomatoes and place them in a bowl. Stir together the oil, brandy, salt, and pepper and pour this dressing over the tomatoes, mixing well. Chill until ready to serve. Spoon into a lettuce-lined bowl and scatter olives and herbs over the salad. Makes 8 servings, about 65 calories each.

Galliano Zabaglione with Peaches

6 egg yolks
6 tablespoons sugar
¼ cup dry white wine
¼ cup Galliano liqueur
1 teaspoon freshly grated lemon
      peel
4 peaches
2 almond macaroons, crumbled

In the top of a double boiler, beat the egg yolks until light, then beat in the sugar, wine, liqueur, and lemon peel. Place over simmering water and beat with a wire whip or portable electric beater until the mixture triples in volume and retains a peak, about 7 minutes. ☆ Have ready 8 wide-bowled wine glasses. Peel and slice peaches into them, then pour in the frothy zabaglione. Sprinkle macaroon crumbs on top. Makes 8 servings, about 125 calories each.

☆ Prepare up to 1 hour in advance to this point for serving chilled.

Summer Dinner from the Côte D'Azur *Serves 6*

Green Bean and Olive Salad
Cherry Tomatoes with Basil
Shrimp and Sole Soufflé
Pears Melba

This eye-catching menu in the French manner calls for bounty from a summer garden. First-of-the-season green beans, cherry tomatoes, leaf lettuce, raspberries, and pears lend freshness. Even if the local grocer supplies these items, it is nice to have a patio herb pot for picking your own parsley, chives, basil, and mint to scent the dishes. A marinated green bean salad is the starting point. Following this is a sole soufflé—a golden puff encasing tiny shrimp. Basil-coated cherry tomatoes spark the plate with color. Sliced Bartlett pears and frosty yogurt drizzled with raspberry sauce make a captivating finish. Present a crisp Muscadet or Johannisberg Riesling as an accompaniment. The calorie count totals about 495 per person for this colorful dinner.

Green Bean and Olive Salad

1 pound small young, slender
     green beans
3 tablespoons olive oil
2 teaspoons Dijon mustard
2 tablespoons white wine vinegar
1 tablespoon finely chopped
     shallots or green onions
½ teaspoon salt
½ pound mushrooms, thinly sliced
1 dozen jumbo pitted ripe olives,
     sliced lengthwise
1 large tomato, peeled, seeded,
     and chopped
1 tablespoon chopped fresh
     parsley
1 tablespoon chopped fresh
     chives
   Butter or leaf lettuce

Trim ends from the green beans and cut lengthwise. Bring 1½ quarts salted water to a boil in a large saucepan. Add the beans and boil uncovered for 5 to 7 minutes, or until crisp tender. Drain and rinse under cold water; drain thoroughly. In a large bowl combine the oil, mustard, vinegar, shallots, and salt. Add the beans and mix lightly, then add the mushrooms and olives. Mix in the tomato, parsley, and chives. Cover and chill for 1 hour before serving. Arrange butter lettuce on 6 salad plates and mound the marinated vegetables on the greens. Makes 6 servings, about 100 calories each.

Cherry Tomatoes with Basil

2 teaspoons butter
3 cups cherry tomatoes, stems
     removed
1 clove garlic, minced
½ teaspoon salt
⅛ teaspoon freshly ground pepper
1 tablespoon chopped fresh basil,
     or ¾ teaspoon crumbled
     dried basil
1 tablespoon chopped fresh
     parsley
1 teaspoon chopped fresh chives
     or green onions

Melt the butter in a large frying pan. Add the tomatoes and garlic and cook 1 to 2 minutes, shaking the pan, just until tomatoes are heated. Sprinkle with salt, pepper, basil, parsley, and chives. Makes 6 servings, about 30 calories each.

Shrimp and Sole Soufflé

½	pound sole or turbot fillets	5	eggs, separated
1	cup water	¾	cup shredded jarlsberg or Swiss cheese
2	tablespoons cornstarch		
1	tablespoon lemon juice	2	ounces small cooked shrimp
½	teaspoon salt	2	tablespoons dry sherry
¼	teaspoon white pepper	2	egg whites
1½	teaspoons Dijon mustard		

Purée the fish with ½ cup of the water in a blender or food processor. Blend the cornstarch with 2 tablespoons of the water. Heat the remaining water with the lemon juice, salt, pepper, and mustard. Stir in the cornstarch paste and cook until thickened. Add this to the fish purée and blend smooth. Return the mixture to the stove and cook 1 minute. Remove from heat and add the egg yolks and half (⅜ cup) of the cheese. Toss the shrimp in sherry to coat them; set aside. Beat the 7 egg whites until stiff. Fold one-third of the whites into the fish mixture, then fold in the remaining whites. Turn into a buttered 10-inch round baking dish. Scatter the shrimp on top and sprinkle with the remaining cheese. Bake in a 400° oven for 20 to 25 minutes, or until set. Makes 6 servings, about 225 calories each.

Pears Melba

1½	cups raspberries
4	fresh pears
1	pint frozen raspberry yogurt
	Mint sprigs

Purée the raspberries in a blender or food processor, then push through a wire strainer to remove the seeds. Core the pears, cut them into wedges, and arrange in dessert bowls. Add a small scoop of frozen yogurt, top with the raspberry purée, and garnish with mint. Makes 6 servings, about 140 calories each.

Summer Smörgasbord *Serves 8*

Pickled Herring in Mushroom Caps
Apple Coleslaw
Pickled Beets
Veal Tongue Platter
Strawberry-Raspberry Soup

Specialties of the Danish kitchen punctuate this summer meal. For a charming appetizer, bits of herring nestle in mushroom caps. Sliced veal tongue, served hot or chilled, is lean yet succulent paired with a zesty sauce or two. Coleslaw and pickled beets are fine accompaniments, and a cool berry soup is a pleasant summertime conclusion. A Grey Riesling or Semillon suits this occasion. The total count is about 450 calories per person for this Danish dinner.

Pickled Herring in Mushroom Caps

24 medium mushroom caps
2 tablespoons plain yogurt
1 can (3½ ounces) pickled herring
   snacks
   Chopped fresh chives or green
   onions

Remove stems from the mushrooms (save them for another purpose). Put ¼ teaspoon of yogurt in each cap. Add a small piece of herring. Sprinkle with chives and chill. Makes 2 dozen appetizers, about 10 calories each.

Apple Coleslaw

⅓ cup sour cream
⅓ cup plain yogurt
1 tablespoon lemon juice
1 teaspoon brown sugar
½ teaspoon salt
  Generous dash of freshly
    ground pepper
6 cups finely shredded cabbage
2 red apples

Mix together the sour cream, yogurt, lemon juice, sugar, salt, and pepper in a large bowl. Add the cabbage, mix lightly, and chill. Just before serving, halve, core, and dice the apples and mix them in. Makes 8 servings, about 65 calories each.

Pickled Beets

1 tablespoon sugar
½ teaspoon dry mustard
½ teaspoon salt
8 whole cloves
1 clove garlic, peeled and
    chopped
⅓ cup cider vinegar
¼ cup water
2 cups sliced cooked fresh beets
    or drained canned beets
1 sweet red onion, sliced into
    rings

Combine the sugar, mustard, salt, cloves, garlic, vinegar, and water in a saucepan. Bring to a boil and then pour it over the beets and onion rings. Cover and chill at least 1 day. ☆ Makes 8 servings, about 15 calories each.

☆ This dish may be prepared up to 1 week in advance to this point.

Veal Tongue Platter

6   veal tongues (about 2 pounds)
1   onion, stuck with 3 cloves
3   to 5 peppercorns
¼   cup fresh celery leaves, or
      ½ teaspoon celery salt
2   chicken bouillon cubes
     Dijon mustard
     Horseradish Sauce (see below)
     Caper Sauce (see below)

Place the tongues in a pan with 1 quart water, the onion, peppercorns, celery leaves, and bouillon cubes. Cover and simmer for 1 to 1½ hours, or until tender. Remove to a platter and let cool slightly, then skin. Reserve broth for soup stock. Slice each on the diagonal and serve hot with one or more sauces. Or, if desired, cool the tongues whole and serve chilled. Makes 8 servings, about 200 calories each.

Horseradish Sauce: Blend together ½ cup plain yogurt, ¼ cup sour cream, 3 tablespoons bottled horseradish sauce, and salt and pepper to taste. Makes about 1 cup. About 18 calories per tablespoon.

Caper Sauce: Blend together ½ cup plain yogurt, ¼ cup sour cream, 1 tablespoon Dijon mustard, 2 tablespoons chopped fresh parsley, 2 tablespoons chopped fresh chives, 1 tablespoon chopped capers, dash lemon juice, and salt and pepper to taste. Makes about 1 cup. About 18 calories per tablespoon.

Strawberry-Raspberry Soup

3   cups strawberries
3   cups raspberries
⅓   cup granulated sugar
2   tablespoons cornstarch
¾   cup water
1   tablespoon lemon juice
¼   cup sour cream
¼   cup plain yogurt
1   teaspoon powdered sugar
½   teaspoon vanilla

Hull and halve the strawberries. Place the strawberries, raspberries, and granulated sugar in a large saucepan and let stand 15 minutes for juices to exude. Heat over low heat to boiling. Mix together the cornstarch and water and stir in. Stirring constantly, boil until the fruits soften and the soup is clear and thickened. Remove from heat and stir in the lemon juice. Chill. ☆ Spoon into small dessert bowls. Just before serving, blend together the sour cream, yogurt, powdered sugar, and vanilla and put a dollop on each bowlful. Makes 8 servings, about 100 calories each.

☆ The soup may be prepared 1 day in advance to this point.

Trattoria Dinner from Bologna Serves 6

Vegetable Platter Salad with Pesto Sauce
Eggplant and Tomato Bisque
Mushrooms Bolognese
Marsala-Kissed Berry and Orange Bowl

The friendly elements of family-style Northern Italian dining characterize this make-ahead dinner. Fresh basil from the garden and pesto sauce from the freezer enhance several dishes. The menu revolves around several typical Mediterranean vegetables—tomatoes, peppers, green onions, egg-plant, carrots, and mushrooms. The vegetable-laden meat sauce gains a new dimension when served with pork instead of the usual beef. Berries and oranges interlaced with Marsala are a cool dessert. Out of season, offer Comice Pears with Gorgonzola or pineapple fingers with provolone. Serve a bottle of Gamay Rosé or White Zinfandel for a treat. The calorie count for this Italian dinner is about 400 per person.

Vegetable Platter Salad with Pesto Sauce

4   large tomatoes, sliced
3   green onions, chopped
1   red or green pepper, seeded
     and cut into strips
2   tablespoons chopped fresh
     parsley
1   tablespoon red wine vinegar
3   tablespoons Pesto Sauce
     (see next page)
½   teaspoon salt
     Generous dash of freshly
     ground pepper

Arrange tomatoes on a platter and scatter the onions, pepper, and parsley on top. Season with vinegar, pesto sauce, salt, and pepper. Makes 6 servings, about 30 calories each.

Pesto Sauce: Place 1½ cups fresh basil leaves, lightly packed, 2 cloves garlic, minced. 2 tablespoons parsley sprigs, ½ teaspoon salt, ⅛ teaspoon freshly ground pepper, and 3 tablespoons freshly grated Parmesan cheese in a food processor and process until finely minced. Turn into a serving dish, cover, and chill. To prevent the surface from darkening, spoon a light film of olive oil over the top. ☆ Chill until ready to serve and then mix in the oil coating. Makes about ½ cup. About 12 calories per tablespoon.

☆ The sauce may be prepared in advance to this point and either frozen or refrigerated.

Eggplant and Tomato Bisque

1 **large onion, finely chopped**
1 **small eggplant**
1 **cup puréed Italian plum
      tomatoes, or about 2 large
      ripe tomatoes**
3 **cups chicken stock (see
      page 26)**
½ **teaspoon salt**
¼ **teaspoon freshly ground pepper**
1 **clove garlic, chopped
      Freshly chopped basil**

Place the onion in a heavy saucepot and let cook in a dry pan over medium-low heat, stirring occasionally. Cut the eggplant into wedges, sprinkle with salt, and let stand 15 minutes for the juices to exude. Rinse, peel, and chop. Add it to the onions, along with the tomatoes, chicken stock, salt, pepper, and garlic. Cover and simmer 10 minutes, or until eggplant is tender. Purée in a blender or food processor. Return to pan and reheat. Ladle into bowls and garnish with basil. If you prefer, add a dollop of Pesto Sauce (see preceding recipe) instead. Makes 6 servings, about 50 calories each.

Mushrooms Bolognese

Bolognese Meat Sauce (see
  below)
1 pound mushrooms
2 tablespoons butter
2 cloves garlic, minced
¼ cup freshly grated Parmesan
  cheese

First prepare the Bolognese Meat Sauce. Slice mushrooms and sauté quickly in butter with garlic just until glazed. Turn into 6 greased ramekins. Spoon in some meat sauce and sprinkle with the cheese. Slip under the broiler until cheese melts. Makes 6 servings, about 250 calories each.

Bolognese Meat Sauce: Using a dry Dutch oven, sauté 2 large onions, chopped, over medium-high heat until soft and starting to brown. Add 3 large shredded carrots and cook several minutes. In a frying pan brown 1 pound lean pork, stirring until crumbly, then add it to the vegetables. Add 1 can (1 pound) ground plum tomatoes, ⅓ cup red wine vinegar, 1½ cups chicken stock, salt and pepper to taste, and 2 cloves garlic, minced. Cover and simmer for 2 hours, letting juices boil down at the end. ☆ Makes about 1¼ quarts meat sauce.

☆ Prepare up to 2 days in advance to this point and refrigerate, or double the quantities and freeze.

Marsala-Kissed Berry and Orange Bowl

3 oranges
2 tablespoons sugar
2 tablespoons sweet Marsala
1 pint strawberries
  Mint sprigs

Grate the peel of 1 orange and then ream the orange for the juice. Mash the peel with sugar to extract the oils. Add the wine and orange juice and mix well. Peel and quarter the other 2 oranges. Hull and halve the berries, if large. Add the sliced oranges and berries to the wine mixture, cover, and chill for 1 hour or longer. Serve in dessert bowls, garnished with mint sprigs. Makes 6 servings, about 70 calories each.

Djakarta Dinner *Serves 6*

Fresh Coconut Appetizers
Peppercorn and Watercress Salad
Indonesian Sate
Asparagus with Peanut Sauce
Baked Papaya with Vanilla Bean

This Far Eastern dinner tantalizes with its spicy overtones. The Indonesian skewered meat is seasoned with coriander. For a truly fresh aroma, the seeds are preferable to the ground spice. Use a spice mill, pepper mill, or coffee grinder to powder them. Fresh coconut chunks introduce the meal and hot baked papaya laced with coconut milk is the finale. A Gewürztraminer would suit this fare. The calorie count for this barbecue is about 405 per person.

Fresh Coconut Appetizers

1   **coconut**
1   **lime, cut in wedges**
    Freshly ground nutmeg

Select a fresh coconut, shaking it to see that it contains lots of liquid, and refrigerate it until ready to use. To crack the coconut open and save the milky fluid, puncture one or two of the three spots on the shell, using an ice pick or small screwdriver, and drain the liquid into a container. Save the milk for the papaya dessert. Heat the coconut on a baking pan in a 350° oven for 30 minutes. Then crack it open and the meat will separate easily from the shell. Cut meat into ½-inch pieces. Serve on a platter, garnished with lime wedges and sprinkled with nutmeg. If desired, toast the coconut slices in a 350° oven for 15 minutes, or until lightly browned. Makes about 3 dozen appetizers, about 10 calories each.

Peppercorn and Watercress Salad

½ teaspoon hot peppercorns
1 teaspoon sesame paste (tahini)
⅓ cup soy sauce
2 teaspoons sesame oil
2 tablespoons cider vinegar
2 teaspoons sugar
1 clove garlic, minced
   Dash of liquid hot pepper
     seasoning
2 to 3 slices peeled fresh ginger
   root, cut into slivers
2 bunches watercress, coarsely
   chopped
½ pound mushrooms, thinly sliced

Using a dry frying pan, roast the peppercorns for 5 minutes over low heat, shaking the pan often. Remove from heat and crush in a mortar and pestle or grind in a pepper grinder. In a serving bowl, mix together the peppercorns, sesame paste, soy, sesame oil, vinegar, sugar, garlic, pepper seasoning and ginger root. Add the watercress and mushrooms and mix lightly. Makes 6 servings, about 35 calories each.

Indonesian Sate

1½ pounds boneless chicken breast,
    leg of lamb,
    or lean pork cubes
1 medium onion, chopped
4 teaspoons freshly ground
    coriander seeds
    Dash of cayenne
2 tablespoons brown sugar
2 cloves garlic, minced
1 teaspoon salt
1 teaspoon black pepper
3 tablespoons lemon juice
¼ cup soy sauce
    Sate Sauce (see below)

Cut the meat into 1-inch cubes. Place in a mixing bowl the onion, coriander, cayenne, sugar, garlic, salt, pepper, lemon juice, and soy; mix well. Add the meat, stir to coat, cover, and chill overnight, stirring occasionally. Thread the meat on skewers and broil or barbecue over medium coals until cooked to taste. Serve with Sate Sauce. Makes 6 servings, about 230 calories each.

Sate Sauce: Sauté ¼ teaspoon cumin, ¼ teaspoon coriander, ¼ teaspoon turmeric, and ¼ teaspoon pepper in ½ teaspoon butter, stirring for 2 minutes. Add 2 tablespoons peanut butter, 1 teaspoon lemon juice, ¼ cup water, ½ teaspoon brown sugar, 1 small clove garlic, minced, and 1 tablespoon chopped shallot or green onion. Season with salt and a dash of liquid hot pepper seasoning. Store any leftover sauce in the refrigerator, covered; it keeps 2 to 3 months. About 30 calories per tablespoon.

Asparagus with Peanut Sauce

1½ pounds asparagus, cauliflower,
        or broccoli
 ⅓ cup soy sauce
 1 clove garlic, minced
 1 green onion, chopped
 2 tablespoons peanut butter
    Dash of liquid hot pepper
        seasoning

Trim and peel the asparagus. Steam in boiling salted water until crisp tender; drain. Turn onto a platter and keep warm. While the asparagus is cooking, combine soy, garlic, onion, and peanut butter in a small saucepan and heat until blended, stirring frequently. Add the liquid hot pepper seasoning and spoon this sauce over the asparagus. Makes 6 servings, about 60 calories each.

Baked Papaya with Vanilla Bean

 3 small papaya
 1 piece (6 inches) vanilla bean
 ½ cup fresh coconut milk
 1 lime, cut in wedges
    Flower blossoms

Halve the papaya and scoop out the seeds. Place the halves on a baking pan. Cut the vanilla bean into 1-inch lengths and split open, scraping a few seed pods into each papaya half and dropping in a piece of the bean as well. Spoon in some coconut milk. Cover with foil. Bake in a 375° oven for 10 to 15 minutes, or until heated. Serve each half on a dessert plate, garnished with a wedge of lime and a blossom from the garden. Makes 6 servings, about 50 calories each.

Gala Party Dinners

An Armenian Feast • Mediterranean Fish
Dinner • French Party Dinner • Cretan
Barbecue • A Celebration Dinner • Egyptian
Barbecue • Moroccan Party Dinner •
Provençal Dinner • A Viennese Dinner

An Armenian Feast Serves 6

Stuffed Grape Leaves with Yogurt Sauce
Veal Boerek
Grilled Vegetables
Bosporus Fruit Salad

The flavors of this party dinner are from the Middle East, where grape leaves, filo-wrapped entrées, yogurt, and a candy made from sesame seed, called halvah, *are commonplace. The menu lends itself to make-ahead preparation. The inviting veal packets can be assembled early and refrigerated, to be baked at the last minute, or they can be baked ahead of time and reheated. A refreshing fruit salad makes a fine accent. Offer a small sweetmeat for dessert, such as halvah, which comes in several flavors— vanilla, chocolate marble, or nut. Fresh dates, perhaps stuffed with a pecan, or commercial honeyed or cinnamon-spiced almonds would also be excellent. Offer a Gamay Beaujolais or a Ruby Cabernet. The calorie count for this dinner is about 535 per person.*

Stuffed Grape Leaves with Yogurt Sauce

1 dozen stuffed grape leaves (see
    page 165)
1 cup plain yogurt
½ teaspoon freshly grated lemon
    peel
½ cup finely diced tomatoes
½ cup finely diced cucumbers
2 tablespoons chopped fresh
    parsley
4 Mediterranean olives, chopped

Steam the stuffed grape leaves until hot. Place 2 on each salad plate. Mix together the yogurt, lemon peel, tomatoes, cucumbers, parsley, and olives and spoon on top. Makes 6 servings, about 80 calories each.

Veal Boerek

1	large onion, chopped	1	egg
2	carrots, peeled and shredded	3	tablespoons chopped fresh parsley
2	cloves garlic, minced		
½	teaspoon allspice	1	teaspoon salt
½	teaspoon coriander	¾	cup freshly grated Parmesan or Romano cheese
⅛	teaspoon freshly ground pepper		
2	medium zucchini, shredded	6	sheets filo dough
1	pound ground veal	1½	tablespoons melted butter

Place the onion in a large dry frying pan over medium heat and cook 5 to 10 minutes, stirring occasionally. Add the carrots, garlic, allspice, coriander, and pepper and cook 5 minutes longer, stirring. Wrap the shredded zucchini in paper towels and squeeze out the moisture, then add it to the pan. Mix together in a large bowl the meat, egg, parsley, salt, cheese, and cooked vegetables. Lay out one sheet of filo dough, brush half of it lightly with melted butter (using 2 brush strokes), and fold it in half. Divide the meat mixture into 6 portions. Place 1 of the round patties in the lower third of the filo piece. Fold the larger dough piece over the meat, not quite covering it completely, making an 8-inch square (approximately). Brush the filo edges lightly with butter and fold in all four corners, meeting in the center. This makes a square packet of meat-filled pastry with a design of 4 triangles on top. Repeat with each filo sheet. Brush lightly with butter. ☆ Place on a baking sheet and bake in a 425° oven for 15 to 20 minutes, or until golden brown. Makes 6 servings, about 250 calories each.

☆ Prepare in advance to this point and freeze. Thaw before baking.

Grilled Vegetables

2 large onions
3 medium tomatoes
1 green pepper
2 teaspoons olive oil
   Salt

Cut the onions into quarters and separate the layers. Wrap the pieces in foil and bake in a 425° oven (or place on barbecue coals) for 20 minutes. Unwrap and scatter in a broiling pan lined with foil. Halve the tomatoes and arrange cut side down in the pan. Seed the pepper and cut into 6 equal pieces; place these in the pan. Drizzle the vegetables with oil and sprinkle with salt. Broil until the vegetables are lightly browned on the edges. Serve each person a tomato half, pepper strip, and several onion slices. Makes 6 servings, about 40 calories each.

Bosporus Fruit Salad

3 large oranges, peeled and thinly sliced
1 cup seedless grapes
1 cup red grapes, halved and seeded
1 cup watercress leaves
1 large Bermuda onion, thinly sliced

¾ cup feta cheese, broken into chunks
3 tablespoons olive oil
1½ tablespoons lemon juice
½ teaspoon salt
   Generous dash of freshly ground pepper
2 tablespoons finely chopped mint

Place the oranges, grapes, watercress, onion, and cheese in a bowl. Mix together the oil, lemon juice, salt, pepper, and mint and pour it over the fruit. Mix lightly. Makes 6 servings, about 165 calories each.

Mediterranean Fish Dinner

Serves 6

Endive and Citrus Salad
Mushrooms in Garlic Butter
Fish Soufflé Florentine
Peach Filbert Tart

There are surprises galore in this festive fish dinner. The starter is a sprightly salad of lime, orange, pistachios, and endive. Sautéed mushrooms and a cloud-light soufflé on a bed of sole and spinach are the entrée. For dessert there is a nut-crusted tart shell replete with a pinwheel of sliced peaches. A Johannisberg Riesling makes a choice wine companion. The calorie count for this gala dinner is about 480 per person.

Endive and Citrus Salad

3 bunches Belgian endive
  Watercress
2 limes, peeled and thinly sliced
2 oranges, peeled and thinly
    sliced
4 tablespoons olive or safflower
    oil
2 tablespoons white wine vinegar
1 tablespoon lemon juice
½ teaspoon freshly grated lemon
    peel
2 tablespoons chopped pistachios

Place sprigs of endive and watercress on individual salad plates. Arrange citrus slices on the greens. For the dressing, mix together well the oil, vinegar, lemon juice, and lemon peel. Spoon this over all and toss. Sprinkle with pistachios. Makes 6 servings, about 150 calories each.

Mushrooms in Garlic Butter

1   tablespoon butter
2   cloves garlic, minced
1   pound mushrooms, sliced
½   teaspoon salt
    Generous dash of freshly
      ground pepper
½   teaspoon crumbled dried
      tarragon
2   tablespoons chopped fresh
      parsley or chives

Using a large frying pan, melt the butter and add the garlic. Add the mushrooms and sauté, stirring. Season with salt, pepper, and tarragon and cook very quickly, about 1 minute. Sprinkle with parsley or chives and remove from pan. Makes 6 servings, about 30 calories each.

Fish Soufflé Florentine

2   green onions or shallots,
      chopped
1   teaspoon butter
1   large bunch spinach, chopped
½   teaspoon salt
¼   teaspoon freshly ground pepper
⅛   teaspoon nutmeg
¼   cup freshly grated Parmesan
      cheese
1¼ pounds sole or turbot fillets
4   eggs, separated
1   teaspoon freshly grated lemon
      peel
½   teaspoon Dijon-style dry
      mustard
⅓   cup sour cream
2   egg whites

Using a large frying pan, sauté the onions in butter until soft. Add the spinach and cook just until it wilts, about 1 minute. Stir in the salt, pepper, and nutmeg and mix in the cheese. Spoon the mixture into a buttered 10-inch baking dish. Season the fillets with more salt and pepper and place on the spinach bed. ☆ Beat egg yolks with lemon peel and mustard until thick and pale yellow. Mix in the sour cream. Beat the 6 egg whites until glossy peaks form and fold into the egg yolk mixture. Spread this over the fish. Bake in a 375° oven for 20 minutes, or until puffed and golden brown. Makes 6 servings, about 200 calories each.

☆ Prepare a few hours in advance to this point and refrigerate.

Peach Filbert Tart

2   frozen puff pastry shells,
      thawed (⅓ of a 10-ounce
      package), or Quick Puff
      Pastry (see page 73)
⅓   cup filberts or almonds
1   tablespoon powdered sugar
1   egg yolk
1½ teaspoons orange liqueur
5   large peaches or nectarines
2   tablespoons apricot jam or
      orange marmalade

Stack puff pastries on a floured board and roll with a rolling pin into a 13- or 14-inch round. Place on a pizza pan and put it in the freezer for 10 minutes to firm up solidly. In the meantime, grind the nuts in a food processor or blender. Add the sugar, egg yolk, and liqueur and process again, mixing well. Prick the pastry with a fork at 2-inch intervals and spread the nut mixture over the pastry, making a thin, even layer. Bake in a 425° oven for 8 minutes, or until golden brown. Let cool. ☆ Just before serving, peel and slice the peaches and arrange them on top of the pastry. Heat the jam until it melts and drizzle it over the fruit. If desired, serve with crème fraîche (see page 57). Makes 8 servings, about 100 calories each.

☆ Prepare in advance to this point and refrigerate.

ℱrench ℘arty ⅅinner   *Serves 6*

Artichoke Heart Salad
Chicken in Terrine en Croûte
Lemon Roof-Tile Cookies

A surprise lends enchantment to a party meal. Here a golden cap of puff pastry seals within a poached chicken and vegetables. The bird is simmered whole, in the French style, then carved at the table. The artichoke and mushroom salad makes a delightfully different first course. Tile-shaped lemon cookies, served with a basket of fresh fruit, are a crispy finish. A Pinot Blanc or dry Chenin Blanc would be a fine accompaniment. For this special occasion dinner, count on about 480 calories per person.

Artichoke Heart Salad

2 packages (8 ounces) frozen artichoke hearts
3 tablespoons olive oil
1½ tablespoons white wine vinegar
2 teaspoons Dijon mustard
1 tablespoon finely chopped shallots
½ teaspoon salt
⅛ teaspoon freshly ground pepper

2 teaspoons fresh chopped tarragon, or ½ teaspoon dried tarragon
½ pound mushrooms, thinly sliced
1 dozen Mediterranean olives, sliced lengthwise
1 large tomato, peeled and chopped
2 tablespoons chopped fresh parsley
   Butter or leaf lettuce

Cook artichoke hearts in boiling salted water until crisp tender, about 7 minutes; drain well. Blend the oil, vinegar, mustard, shallots, salt, pepper, and tarragon in a bowl. Add the artichoke hearts and mix lightly. Add the mushrooms and olives. Mix in the tomato and parsley. Cover and chill 1 hour before serving. Arrange butter lettuce on 6 salad plates and mound the marinated vegetables on top. Makes 6 servings, about 110 calories each.

Chicken in Terrine en Croûte

1 broiler-fryer (3½ pounds)
2 cloves garlic, minced
3 cups chicken stock (see page 26)
3 carrots, peeled and cut in 1-inch chunks
2 turnips, peeled and cut in wedges
1 dozen small white boiling onions, peeled
½ pound green beans, ends trimmed

2 tablespoons minced parsley
1 tomato, peeled and diced
½ teaspoon salt
  Generous dash freshly ground pepper
5 ounces frozen puff pastry, thawed (½ package or 3 individual pastries), or Quick Puff Pastry (see page 73)
1 egg white, lightly beaten

Remove any excess fat from the chicken and season with a little salt and pepper. Tuck garlic inside the cavity. Place in a roasting pan and roast in a 425° oven for 20 minutes, or until golden brown. In the meantime, bring the chicken stock to a boil and blanch the carrots, turnips, onions, and green beans for 2 minutes. Place the browned chicken in a large bowl for baking or in a deep soufflé dish and surround it with the blanched vegetables, parsley, and tomato. Pour in the chicken stock. Add the salt and pepper. Stack the pastry shells on a lightly floured board and roll out dough to a round 2 inches larger than the diameter of the bowl. Brush the pastry with egg white and arrange it, brushed side down, over the bowl, bringing pastry edge ½ inch down the outside rim of the dish. ☆ Brush top with remaining egg white. Bake in a 425° oven for 45 minutes; reduce temperature to 375° and bake 30 minutes longer. Turn off the oven and let it stand 15 minutes longer. If necessary, cover the top with foil to prevent overbrowning. To serve, use a small knife to cut out the crust and lift it off. Take out the chicken and carve. Serve chicken with vegetables and a wedge of crust. Makes 6 servings, about 300 calories each.

☆ Prepare in advance to this point and refrigerate. Increase baking time by 10 to 15 minutes.

Lemon Roof-Tile Cookies

3½ tablespoons soft butter
½ cup sugar
2 egg whites
5 tablespoons cake flour
⅓ cup blanched almonds, finely
    ground
¼ teaspoon lemon extract
1 teaspoon freshly grated lemon
    peel
3 tablespoons slivered almonds

Beat together the butter and sugar until light and fluffy. Add the egg whites and beat a few seconds more. Sift the flour, remeasure, and stir it into the batter all at once. Fold in the ground almonds, lemon extract, and lemon peel. Grease 3 cookie sheets. Drop the batter by half-teaspoonfuls at least 4 inches apart onto the cookie sheets. Spread into 3-inch circles with the back of a spoon. (Batter will be thin and open in spots.) Sprinkle each cookie with a few slivered almonds. Bake in a 425° oven for 4 minutes, or until golden brown. Remove from baking sheets immediately and drape over a rolling pin, forming a "tile" shape. ☆ Makes 2 dozen cookies, about 40 calories each.

☆ Cookies may be made several days in advance to this point; store in an airtight container.

$\mathcal{C}retan\;\mathcal{B}arbecue$ Serves 6

Cumin Dip with Garden Relishes
Clam Soup Avgolemono
Spanakopita
Souvlakia
Peaches in Burgundy

A barbecue starring souvlakia, or Greek lamb kebabs, offers a festive menu that readily adapts to both long and short guest lists. Meze prelude a Middle Eastern party meal. Here a yogurt sauce sparked with cumin and chives is the dip for a bounty of fresh garden relishes. The soup is a clam broth thickened with lemon and egg. In the Greek kitchen the dishes are often prepared in advance for serving cold, warm, or hot, a style of dining that is well-suited to summer's unpredictable weather. Spanakopita, or spinach pie, is one example; it is superb at any temperature. The charcoal-broiled lamb kebabs are at their best when first marinated overnight. First-of-the season peaches, sliced and steeped in Burgundy, are a light finale. A Petite Sirah or Pinot Noir makes a choice wine accompaniment. The approximate calorie count totals 615 per person for this summer barbecue.

Cumin Dip with Garden Relishes

1 green onion, chopped	1 tablespoon chopped fresh parsley
½ teaspoon cumin	1 tablespoon chopped fresh chives
¼ teaspoon butter	
¾ cup plain yogurt	Assorted relishes
¼ teaspoon salt	
⅛ teaspoon freshly ground pepper	

Using a small frying pan, sauté the onion and cumin in butter for 2 minutes to remove the raw taste of the spice. Stir in the yogurt, salt, pepper, parsley, and chives. Turn into a sauce bowl and chill. Pass with a basket or platter of assorted relishes, such as cherry tomatoes, cucumber fingers, carrot sticks, pea pods, and mushrooms. Makes about 1 cup. About 9 calories per tablespoon. Makes 6 servings, about 30 calories each, with the crudités.

Clam Soup Avgolemono

1   bottle (8 ounces) clam juice
1   can (7 ounces) minced clams,
      drained (reserve liquid)
$1\frac{1}{2}$ cups water
1   chicken bouillon cube
3   eggs
3   tablespoons lemon juice
$\frac{1}{4}$ teaspoon salt
    Generous dash of freshly
      ground pepper
2   tablespoons minced fresh
      parsley

Using a large saucepot, heat together the clam juice, the liquid from the canned clams, the water, and the bouillon cube until boiling. Beat eggs until blended and beat in the lemon juice. Blend a little of the hot broth with the egg-lemon mixture, then pour all the egg-lemon into the pan containing the remaining broth. Cook over very low heat, stirring, until thickened slightly, or until the soup coats a spoon. Add the clams and season with the salt and pepper. ☆ Ladle into small bowls or cups and sprinkle with parsley. Makes 6 servings, about 100 calories each.

☆ The soup may be prepared in advance to this point and refrigerated. Reheat slowly, without boiling.

Spanakopita

1 bunch green onions, chopped
1 tablespoon melted butter
1 pound spinach with stems,
   finely chopped
½ cup chopped fresh parsley
2 eggs
2 ounces feta cheese, crumbled
¼ cup freshly grated Romano or
   Parmesan cheese (about
   1 ounce)
½ teaspoon salt
¼ teaspoon freshly ground pepper
¼ teaspoon dried oregano
4 sheets filo dough

Sauté the onions in ½ teaspoon of the butter until soft. Place the spinach and parsley in a towel and squeeze to remove excess moisture. Beat eggs until blended and mix in onions, greens, cheese, salt, pepper, and oregano. Lay out 1 sheet filo, brush lightly with melted butter and cover with 3 more sheets of filo, brushing each with butter. Spoon filling in a ribbon down a long side. Fold the short sides in 1 inch, and roll up. Place on a greased baking pan. Brush the top with remaining melted butter. Bake in a 375° oven for 30 minutes, or until crisp and brown. Cut into 2-inch pieces and serve hot or cold. ☆ Makes 6 servings, about 125 calories each.

☆ Prepare 1 day in advance to this point. Reheat in a 375° oven for 20 minutes, or until hot.

Souvlakia

$1\frac{1}{2}$ pounds boneless leg of lamb,
        cut into $1\frac{1}{2}$-inch cubes
$\frac{1}{3}$ cup lemon juice
1 tablespoon olive oil
1 teaspoon salt
1 teaspoon oregano
2 cloves garlic, minced
2 green onions, chopped
$\frac{1}{4}$ teaspoon freshly ground pepper
1 green pepper, cut into $1\frac{1}{4}$-inch
        pieces
1 medium white onion, cut into
        sixths

Place the meat in a large bowl. Mix together the lemon juice, oil, salt,
oregano, garlic, pepper, and onions and pour this over the lamb. Cover
and chill several hours or overnight, stirring several times. Thread meat
on skewers, alternating with pieces of green pepper and onion. Barbecue
over medium-hot coals or broil, basting often with marinade and turning
to brown all sides. Cook about 15 minutes for medium-rare meat. Makes 6
servings, about 260 calories each.

Peaches in Burgundy

6 large peaches
2 teaspoons sugar
2 cups Burgundy or Zinfandel

Just before serving, peel and slice the peaches into large-bowled wine
glasses. Sprinkle lightly with the sugar. Pour in the wine. Makes 6 servings, about 100 calories each.

A Celebration Dinner Serves 6

Filbert Green Salad
Roast Lamb Dijon
Shredded Vegetable Trio
Strawberry Orange Sorbet

For a celebration dinner, a boned and rolled leg of lamb sheathed with Dijon mustard and soy sauce provides a spectacular entrée. Cooked in the French manner, still juicy-pink within, it is delicious paired with a trio of color-keyed shredded vegetables. A butter lettuce salad with toasted filberts and chopped chicken livers is an excellent dinner partner. For dessert, a food processor makes fast work of turning out a fluffy strawberry sorbet. An aged Pinot Noir complements this menu. The calorie count totals about 555 per person for this roast lamb dinner.

Filbert Green Salad

2 heads butter lettuce
   White Wine Vinegar Dressing
     (see below)
3 tablespoons chopped toasted
     filberts
2 sieved egg yolks
2 cooked chicken livers, finely
     diced

Wash and dry the lettuce, tear it into bite-sized pieces, and place in a salad bowl. Pour in the dressing and mix well. Scatter the nuts, sieved egg yolk, and chopped livers on top; toss lightly. Spoon onto salad plates. Makes 6 servings, about 125 calories each.

White Wine Vinegar Dressing: Place in a small jar 4 tablespoons safflower or olive oil, 1½ tablespoons white wine vinegar, 1 tablespoon lemon juice, ½ teaspoon salt, 2 teaspoons Dijon mustard, and ½ teaspoon crumbled dried tarragon. Shake well.

Roast Lamb Dijon

½ cup Dijon mustard
2 tablespoons soy sauce
2 cloves garlic, minced
1 teaspoon chopped peeled fresh
   ginger root
1 leg of lamb (5 pounds), boned,
   rolled, and tied
  Mint or rosemary sprigs

For the coating, mix together the mustard, soy, garlic, and ginger and rub this on the outside of the lamb roast. Place the meat on a rack in a roasting pan. Chill 4 hours for seasonings to permeate meat. Roast in a 350° oven until a meat thermometer registers 160° to 165° for medium-rare meat, or about 1 to 1¼ hours. Place on a board for carving and ring the leg with whole fresh mint or rosemary. Makes 6 servings, about 300 calories each.

Shredded Vegetable Trio

Select three seasonal vegetables with an eye to color contrast, such as carrots, cauliflower, yellow crookneck squash, zucchini, broccoli and turnips. Place cooked shredded vegetables on a platter in separate sections. Makes 6 servings, about 75 calories each.

Shredded Carrots: Peel and shred 6 medium carrots. Place in a saucepan with 2 tablespoons water, salt and pepper to taste, a dash of nutmeg, and 1 teaspoon butter. Cover and simmer until crisp tender, about 4 to 5 minutes.

Shredded Zucchini: Trim the ends from 3 medium zucchini and shred. Place in a saucepan with 1 teaspoon butter, salt and pepper to taste, and 2 teaspoons fresh chopped basil. Cook until crisp tender, about 2 to 3 minutes.

Shredded Turnips: Peel 3 to 4 turnips and shred. Place in a saucepan with 2 tablespoons water, 1 teaspoon butter, and salt and pepper to taste. Simmer 3 to 4 minutes or until crisp tender. Sprinkle with 1 tablespoon chopped chives.

Strawberry Orange Sorbet

4 cups strawberries, hulled
½ cup orange juice
2 tablespoons honey

Purée the strawberries with the orange juice and honey, using a food processor or blender. Pour into a shallow pan and freeze until firm but not solid, about 1½ hours. Spoon about half into a food processor and blend until fluffy; repeat with remainder. (Without a food processor, spoon ice into the bowl of an electric mixer and beat, starting on low speed, until smooth and fluffy.) Turn into a freezer container and freeze until firm. ☆ Makes 6 servings, about 55 calories each.

☆ The sorbet may be prepared 2 weeks in advance to this point.

Egyptian Barbecue

Grilled Scampi with Herbs
Cold Cucumber Soup
Chicken Brochettes Alexandria
Broiled Eggplant Sesame
Apricot and Pistachio Soufflé

For a sophisticated take-off on Egyptian dining, consider these spicy and intriguing dishes. To honor King Tut's visit to the United States, this cuisine is quite apropos. As in most Middle Eastern countries, many plates of meze begin the meal. In Cairo it might be beautiful grilled scampi from the Red Sea. Next, introduce a refreshingly cool cucumber soup, which is also excellent hot. Barbecue kebabs of golden spiced chicken, red peppers, and tiny onions and grill slices of sesame-basted eggplant for the main course. For the finale, an apricot soufflé is dusted with salted green pistachios. Pour a Cabernet Blanc or Sylvaner for a superb companion. The calorie count for this summer barbecue is 445 per person.

Grilled Scampi with Herbs

3 tablespoons lemon juice	1 teaspoon crumbled dried oregano
1 tablespoon dry vermouth	
1 tablespoon olive oil	½ teaspoon salt
2 cloves garlic, minced	Generous dash of freshly ground pepper
1 tablespoon chopped fresh parsley	1 pound large fresh shrimp (18 to a pound)
1 green onion, chopped	Chopped fresh cilantro

Mix together the lemon juice, vermouth, oil, garlic, parsley, onion, oregano, salt, and pepper. Shell the shrimp bodies, leaving the tail shells intact, and split the shrimp meat half way to the tail, washing out the sand vein. Let marinate in the dressing for 30 minutes. Using wooden skewers, spear 2 or 3 shrimp just above the tail shell. Barbecue over medium-hot coals, turning for 4 to 5 minutes, or until shrimp turn pink and curl up in a butterfly shape. Sprinkle with cilantro. Makes 6 servings, about 75 calories each.

Cold Cucumber Soup

2 large cucumbers, peeled
1 quart chicken stock (see
    page 26)
2 tablespoons white wine vinegar
4 teaspoons fresh dill weed, or
    1 teaspoon dried dill weed
3 tablespoons cornstarch
3 tablespoons cold water
½ cup plain yogurt
¼ cup sour cream
½ teaspoon salt
⅛ teaspoon freshly ground pepper
¼ cup chopped chives

Halve cucumbers lengthwise, remove seeds with a spoon, and dice. Purée with 1 cup of the stock in a blender. Bring the remaining stock and the cucumber purée to a boil, adding the vinegar and dill weed, and simmer for 10 to 15 minutes. Stir in the paste of cornstarch and cold water and cook until thickened, about 2 minutes. Cool. Purée with yogurt and sour cream and season with salt and pepper. Serve garnished with chives or, if desired, add part of the chives to the soup. Makes 8 servings, about 60 calories each.

Chicken Brochettes Alexandria

1½ pounds boned chicken breasts (3 to 4 split breasts)
½ teaspoon butter
1 tablespoon curry powder
½ teaspoon turmeric
½ teaspoon cardamom
½ teaspoon allspice
2 tablespoons plain yogurt
1 tablespoon tahini (sesame seed paste)
1 tablespoon lemon juice
1 tablespoon cider vinegar or white wine vinegar
½ teaspoon salt
12 cherry tomatoes
12 small boiling onions, parboiled
1 red or green pepper, seeded and cut into 1-inch pieces
Watercress

Skin chicken and cut into 1-inch pieces. Melt butter in a small pan and sauté the curry, turmeric, cardamom, and allspice 2 to 3 minutes to eliminate their raw taste. Remove from heat. Mix together the yogurt, tahini, lemon juice, vinegar, sautéed spices, and salt in a large bowl. Add the chicken pieces and let them marinate 30 minutes. Thread chicken on 6 skewers, alternating with tomatoes, onions, and pepper pieces. Broil or barbecue, turning, until lightly browned and completely cooked, about 8 minutes. Serve with a garnish of watercress. If desired, pass yogurt seasoned with chopped chives for a sauce. Makes 6 servings, about 190 calories each.

Broiled Eggplant Sesame

1 large eggplant or 6 small Japanese eggplant
Salt
Freshly ground pepper
1 tablespoon sesame oil

Slice the eggplant into ¾-inch-thick slices. (Or cut the small eggplants in half lengthwise.) Sprinkle generously with salt and let stand 15 minutes for juices to exude. Rinse under cold running water. Season with salt and pepper and brush lightly with sesame oil. Place on a broiling pan and broil (or barbecue) until completely cooked, about 5 to 10 minutes. Makes 6 to 8 servings, about 40 calories each.

Apricot and Pistachio Soufflé

¾ cup dried apricots (about 30 halves)
¾ cup water
½ cup plain yogurt
2 egg whites
   Dash of salt
2 tablespoons orange marmalade
2 tablespoons chopped salted pistachios

Place all but 6 apricot halves in a saucepan, cover with water, and simmer 10 to 15 minutes, or until tender. Chop the reserved 6 apricots. Purée the cooked fruit in a blender or food processor with the yogurt. Beat the egg whites until soft peaks form, then beat in the salt and marmalade, whipping until stiff. Fold one-third of the whites into the apricot purée; fold in the remaining whites and the chopped apricots. Turn into individual soufflé dishes or dessert bowls and chill until set. ☆ Sprinkle with pistachios at serving time. Makes 6 servings, about 80 calories each.

☆ Prepare 1 day in advance to this point.

Moroccan Party Dinner
Serves 8

Tabbuli
Bastilla
Zucchini Medley
Mangos Flambé

The multilayered and savory pastry called bastilla is a star of the Moroccan cuisine. A mix of sweet and spicy, it blends curried eggs, chicken strips, and toasted almonds under cinnamon-dusted filo. By scaling down the butter traditionally used, the dish becomes low-calorie. It can be assembled several hours in advance and refrigerated. Bake and serve at the last minute to show off the excellence of its tissue-thin layers of flaky crust. A cracked wheat and fresh vegetable salad and minted zucchini make fine companions. Blaze mangos for a gala finish. Sip a Sylvaner, Lambrusco, or Rheingau Spätlese wine. The calorie count for this party meal is about 460 per person.

Tabbuli

⅓ cup finely ground cracked
   wheat
1 pound vine-ripened tomatoes
   (about 3 medium)
1 cup chopped fresh parsley
3 green onions, finely chopped
2 tablespoons chopped fresh mint
½ cup diced seeded cucumber

1 small red or green pepper,
   seeded and diced
4 tablespoons olive oil
3 tablespoons lemon juice
¾ teaspoon salt
¼ teaspoon freshly ground pepper
½ teaspoon sumak* (optional)
½ teaspoon allspice
   Romaine or grape leaves

Place wheat in a bowl. Halve the tomatoes and squeeze the juice over the wheat, stirring to mix. Let stand while preparing the other ingredients. Chop the squeezed tomatoes and toss with the parsley, onions, mint, cucumber, and diced pepper. Add to the wheat. For the dressing, combine the oil, lemon juice, salt, pepper, sumak, and allspice and pour over the

* Sumak is a tart spice available in Middle Eastern grocery stores. Without it increase the lemon juice slightly.

wheat and vegetable mixture. Mix lightly. Line a platter with grape leaves or Romaine and mound the salad in the center. Pass additional grape or Romaine leaves for scooping up the salad. Makes 8 servings, about 110 calories each.

Bastilla

4 tablespoons butter
1½ teaspoons ginger
1 teaspoon cumin
½ teaspoon turmeric
½ teaspoon allspice
¼ teaspoon cayenne
2 teaspoons cinnamon
1 large onion, finely chopped
5 large split chicken breasts
    (about 2½ pounds)
1 teaspoon salt
3 tablespoons chopped fresh
    parsley
2 tablespoons chopped cilantro
½ cup water
8 eggs
6 sheets filo dough
1 tablespoon powdered sugar
⅓ cup toasted slivered blanched
    almonds

Melt 1 tablespoon of the butter in a large frying pan and sauté the ginger, cumin, turmeric, allspice, cayenne, and 1 teaspoon of the cinnamon for 2 minutes, stirring, to remove their raw taste. Add the onion and sauté until soft. Skin the chicken breasts and place them in the pan, turning to coat with spices. Add the parsley, cilantro, and water. Cover and simmer 15 minutes. Let cool. Bone the chicken and cut into bite-sized strips;

reserve pan juices. Beat the eggs until blended, then beat in the reserved juices. Melt another 1 tablespoon of the butter in a large frying pan and scramble the eggs softly. Let cool. Melt the remaining 2 tablespoons butter. Brush the bottom of a 14-inch pizza or other baking pan with the melted butter and place on it, one at a time, 3 sheets filo, buttering each one very lightly and overlapping them irregularly, forming a 12-inch round. Spoon eggs on top of filo. Cover with chicken strips. Mix the powdered sugar with the remaining 1 teaspoon cinnamon and mix half of it with the nuts. Scatter the almonds over the chicken. Fold the filo corners over the filling. Cover with 1 whole sheet of filo, tucking its edges underneath. Brush with melted butter. Cover with remaining 2 sheets of filo, again tucking in corners and brushing with butter. Bake in a 425° oven for 20 minutes, or until golden brown. Let cool a few minutes. Dust the remaining cinnamon sugar over the top. With a knife, score through the sugar, making a diamond pattern. Makes 8 servings, about 250 calories each.

Zucchini Medley

½ teaspoon olive oil
6 medium zucchini, thinly sliced
3 green onions, chopped
2 cloves garlic, minced
3 leaves mint, chopped
1 tomato, peeled and chopped
¾ teaspoon salt
¼ teaspoon freshly ground pepper

Heat a large frying pan with oil and add zucchini, onions, garlic, mint, and tomato. Season with the salt and pepper. Cover and cook over low heat until vegetables are crisp tender, about 7 minutes. Makes 6 servings, about 25 calories each.

Mangos Flambé

3 tablespoons orange marmalade
2 tablespoons lime juice
3 large mangos, peeled and sliced
3 tablespoons brandy or cognac

Combine in a frying pan or flame-proof serving dish the marmalade and lime juice. Add the mangos and cook until hot. Heat the brandy in a small, long-handled pan. Take up a spoonful, ignite it, and pour it over the mangos. Slowly pour in the remaining brandy; when flame dies out, spoon fruit and sauce into dessert bowls. Makes 8 servings, about 75 calories each.

Provençal Dinner   Serves 4

Spring Greens Soup
Braised Leeks
Chicken in Vinegar
Strawberry Crêpes Flambé

Traditional French country dining is at its best here. Fresh greens lace a soup, leeks poach in broth, vinegar punctuates a chicken sauté, and strawberry crêpes are flambéed with Kirsch. It is a pretty menu, offering the spring and summer garden bounty in a sophisticated style. Serve a chilled Chenin Blanc or a Pouilly-Fuissé with the meal. Allow 430 calories per person for this spring dinner.

Spring Greens Soup

2   teaspoons butter
3   green onions, chopped
¾   cup shredded spinach
¾   cup shredded lettuce
⅓   cup chopped watercress
3   tablespoons chopped fresh
      parsley
3   cups chicken stock (see page 26)
2   tablespoons plain yogurt
2   tablespoons sour cream or
      crème fraîche (see page 57)
½   teaspoon salt
⅛   teaspoon freshly ground pepper
      Chopped chives

Melt the butter in a saucepan and sauté the onions until tender. Add the spinach, lettuce, watercress, and parsley; cover and steam 5 minutes. Add stock and simmer 10 minutes. Stir in the yogurt and sour cream. Season with the salt and pepper. Makes 4 servings, about 60 calories each.

Braised Leeks

8 leeks or 1 large bunch
   asparagus
1 cup chicken stock (see page 26)
6 whole allspice
1 tablespoon chopped fresh
   parsley

Trim the root end from leeks, remove tough fibrous outer layers, and trim off the tough green leaves. Split lengthwise. Hold each section under running water and rinse away sand. Lay the leeks in a saucepan, cover with chicken stock, add allspice, and bring to a boil. Cover and simmer 10 to 15 minutes, or until tender. Place leeks on a serving dish. Cook down juices slightly and spoon a few tablespoons over the leeks. Sprinkle with parsley. Makes 4 servings, about 30 calories each.

Chicken in Vinegar

4 large split chicken breasts
   Salt
   Freshly ground pepper
1 teaspoon butter
½ teaspoon crumbled dried
   tarragon
1 shallot, minced
2 cloves garlic, finely chopped

3 tablespoons dry white wine
3 tablespoons white wine vinegar
1 medium tomato, peeled and
   diced
⅓ cup heavy cream
1 tablespoon finely chopped fresh
   chives or parsley

Season the chicken breasts with salt and pepper to taste. Using a large frying pan, sauté the breasts in butter, turning to brown both sides. Add the tarragon, shallot, garlic, and wine. Cover and simmer 15 minutes. Transfer chicken to a heated platter and pour off the pan juices, reserving them. Pour vinegar into the pan and cook down until reduced by half. Add tomato and cook until hot. Pour in the cream and the reserved pan juices, stir, and cook down sauce slightly. Spoon it over chicken and sprinkle with chives or parsley. Makes 4 servings, about 250 calories each.

Strawberry Crêpes Flambé

 4 crêpes (see page 34)
1½ cups strawberries, hulled and
      halved
 2 tablespoons cherry or orange
      liqueur
1½ teaspoons powdered sugar
 8 whole berries

Prepare 4 crêpes. Marinate the halved berries in sugar and 1 tablespoon of the liqueur for 30 minutes at room temperature. Spoon the berries in a ribbon on the crêpes and roll up. Place in a flame-proof serving dish. Dust the top lightly with powdered sugar. To serve, ignite the remaining liqueur and spoon it, flaming, over the crêpes. Garnish with whole berries. Makes 4 servings, about 90 calories each.

$\mathcal{A}$ Viennese Dinner Serves 6

Mushrooms and Watercress in Mustard Dressing
Roast Game Hens with Green Grapes
Broccoli with Prosciutto
Caramelized Pear Tart

This continental menu offers many delights in a lean manner. It is a fine choice for a guest dinner as many dishes may be done well in advance. A wine and mustard dressing binds fresh sliced mushrooms and watercress for a first course. Grapes in a wine sauce cloak game hens, prosciutto with broccoli makes an unusual vegetable course, and poached pears in caramel adorn puff pastry for dessert. A bottle of oak-aged Zinfandel or Merlot would be nice. Allow 450 calories per person.

Mushrooms and Watercress in Mustard Dressing

1   tablespoon olive or safflower
     oil
3   tablespoons red wine vinegar
2   tablespoons Dijon mustard
1   teaspoon crumbled dried
     tarragon
½   teaspoon salt
¼   teaspoon freshly ground pepper
1   tablespoon chopped fresh
     chives
1   pound mushrooms, sliced
1   bunch watercress or butter
     lettuce

For the dressing, mix together well the oil, vinegar, mustard, tarragon, salt, pepper, and chives. Add the mushrooms to the dressing, mixing lightly. Add several sprigs of watercress. Chill briefly. Arrange remaining watercress on a platter and mound the mushroom salad on top. Makes 6 servings, about 35 calories each.

Roast Game Hens with Green Grapes

3 Rock Cornish game hens
   Salt
   Freshly ground pepper
1½ cups seedless grapes
¼ cup dry sherry or vermouth
¾ cup chicken stock (see page 26)
½ teaspoon freshly grated lemon
     peel
1 teaspoon lemon juice
1 teaspoon arrowroot (optional)

Season game hens inside and out with salt and pepper and stuff the cavities with 4 grapes apiece. Place in a roasting pan and roast in a 375° oven for 1 hour, basting occasionally with the sherry, until drumsticks move easily and birds are golden brown. If necessary add a little chicken stock to the pan juices to prevent them from getting too dark. Remove birds to a warm platter. Skim fat from pan juices and stir in remaining chicken stock, lemon peel, and lemon juice. Bring to a boil and add remaining grapes; let juices reduce slightly. If desired, thicken with arrowroot. Cut hens in half and pass the sauce separately. Makes 6 servings, about 225 calories each.

Broccoli with Prosciutto

2 bunches broccoli
1½ teaspoons butter
1½ teaspoons olive oil
3 cloves garlic, minced
4 slices prosciutto, cut in thin
    strips

Cut broccoli into small flowerets, peeling the thick stalks. Steam over simmering water until crisp tender, about 10 to 15 minutes. Meanwhile, heat butter and oil in a small pan. Add the garlic and sauté until golden, then add the prosciutto and heat thoroughly. Add the broccoli and heat, coating with the sauce. Makes 6 servings, about 40 calories each.

Caramelized Pear Tart

2 frozen puff pastry shells,
    thawed (⅓ of a 10-ounce
    package) or Quick Puff Pastry
    (see page 73)
6 large Bartlett pears or tart
    cooking apples, peeled
⅔ cup sugar
⅓ cup water
1 piece (2 inches) split vanilla
    bean

Stack the thawed puff pastries and roll out on a lightly floured board to a 12-inch round. Place in a 10-inch springform pan, letting the edge roll slightly up the sides. Prick with a fork. Place in a freezer for 5 minutes to chill thoroughly. Bake in a 450° oven for 8 to 10 minutes, or until golden brown. (The shell will shrink slightly, completely fitting the bottom of the pan.) ☆ Cut the pears into eight pieces, discarding the cores. Bring ⅓ cup of the sugar and the water to a boil in a large frying pan. Add the fruit and vanilla bean; cover and simmer 10 minutes. Remove cover and continue cooking until the fruit is tender and slightly caramelized and the liquid is evaporated, about 5 to 10 minutes. Remove the vanilla bean. Spoon the fruit into the baked shell. Place the remaining ⅓ cup sugar in a saucepan and heat without stirring (shake the pan instead), over moderately high heat until the sugar melts and turns amber. Immediately pour it over the fruit, making a swirled pattern on top. Let cool slightly, but serve warm. Makes 8 servings, about 150 calories each.

☆ The shell may be prepared 1 to 2 days in advance.

Easy Spontaneous Suppers

Armenian Pizza Supper • Mykonos Soup
Supper • Supper from Normandy • Mandarin
Supper • Elegant French Supper • Supper from
Genoa • Clam Diggers' Sundown Supper •
A Scandinavian Supper • After-Theatre Supper

$\mathcal{A}$rmenian $\mathcal{P}$izza $\mathcal{S}$upper Serves 6

Eggplant and Walnut Spread
Armenian Pizzas
Turkish Cucumber and Grape Salad
Peaches with Honey Lime Cream

Integrating one cuisine with another often pays off in dividends. Here, 12-inch Mexican flour tortillas form the base for instant Armenian lamb pizzas. The result is a crisp-edged, plate-sized entrée in minutes. It makes a captivating spur-of-the-moment summer supper. Round out the main course with a toasted walnut and eggplant spread, swiftly assembled in a food processor. A diced cucumber and grape salad, dressed with yogurt, and honeyed peaches for dessert complete the menu. With the meal pour a Grignolino, Grignolino Rosé, or good red jug wine. About 455 calories per person for this Armenian dinner.

Eggplant and Walnut Spread

1 large eggplant	$\frac{1}{2}$ cup plain yogurt
4 medium mushrooms	4 tablespoons walnuts, toasted
2 green onions, chopped	2 tablespoons chopped fresh
2 tablespoons lemon juice	parsley
3 cloves garlic, chopped	Cherry tomatoes
$\frac{1}{2}$ teaspoon salt	Romaine or grape leaves
$\frac{1}{8}$ teaspoon freshly ground pepper	

Bake the whole eggplant in a baking pan, uncovered, in a 400° oven for 45 minutes, or until soft. Dip into cold water. Prick with a fork and squeeze out the juices, then peel off the skin. Cool. Place the pulp in a blender or food processor with the mushrooms, onions, lemon juice, and garlic. Purée until smooth. Season with the salt and pepper. Stir in the yogurt, nuts, and parsley and blend just until the nuts are finely chopped. Spoon into a bowl and chill. To serve, spread on halved cherry tomatoes and Romaine or grape leaves. Makes about 2 cups. Makes 6 servings, about 80 calories each.

Armenian Pizzas

1¼ pounds ground lamb
1 teaspoon salt
¼ teaspoon freshly ground pepper
2 cloves garlic, minced
½ teaspoon cumin
½ teaspoon allspice
4 green onions, chopped
2 tablespoons pine nuts
⅓ cup tomato sauce
2 egg whites
1 cup freshly grated Monterey
      jack cheese (about 4 ounces)
6 12-inch flour tortillas

Mix together the lamb, salt, pepper, garlic, cumin, allspice, onions, pine nuts, tomato sauce, and egg whites. Lay out each tortilla on a baking sheet (fitting 2 to a sheet) and put some of the meat mixture on each one, covering loosely to within 1½ inches of the edge. Sprinkle with cheese. ☆ Bake in a 425° oven for 10 to 12 minutes, or until meat is browned and the edges are crisp. Makes 6 servings, about 275 calories each.

☆ Prepare in advance to this point.

Turkish Cucumber and Grape Salad

2   medium cucumbers, peeled,
       seeded, and diced
1   cup plain yogurt
1   clove garlic, minced
1   tablespoon distilled white
       vinegar
½   teaspoon salt
⅛   teaspoon freshly ground pepper
1   green onion, finely chopped
3   mint leaves, chopped
1   cup seedless grapes
     Romaine or grape leaves
     Mint sprigs

Sprinkle diced cucumbers with salt and let stand 15 minutes for juices to exude; rinse under running water and pat dry. Mix together in a bowl the yogurt, garlic, vinegar, salt, pepper, onion, and chopped mint. Add the cucumber and grapes and chill. Serve on Romaine or grape leaves and garnish with mint sprigs. Makes 6 servings, about 40 calories each.

Peaches with Honey Lime Cream

6   peaches
2   tablespoons honey
2   tablespoons lime juice
1   teaspoon freshly grated lime
       peel
     Dash of mace or cardamom
     Blossoms

Peel and slice the peaches into a large bowl. Mix together the honey, lime juice, peel, and mace and spoon this over the fruit, mixing lightly. Spoon into dessert bowls and garnish with a flower blossom, such as nasturtium or fuschia. Makes 6 servings, about 60 calories each.

Mykonos Soup Supper Serves 4

Stuffed Grape Leaves
Fish-Stuffed Tomatoes
Sorrel Avgolemono Soup
Stuffed Apricot Platter

Taking liberties with a classic dish often results in a remarkable new taste treat. Here the renowned Greek lemon soup avgolemono is threaded with sorrel and strewn with feta cheese and pistachios. Suddenly a humble side dish becomes the star. Piquant stuffed grape leaves introduce the meal. A fish salad seasoned the Mediterranean way, with olive oil and lemon, follows. Dessert is a fresh fruit platter. A Sauvignon Blanc or Grey Riesling suits the occasion. Count on about 485 calories per person for this Mediterranean supper.

Stuffed Grape Leaves

3 to 4 dozen fresh or canned
    grape leaves
1 large onion, finely chopped
2 tablespoons olive oil
1 cup short-grain rice
¼ cup finely chopped fresh
    parsley
2 tablespoons chopped fresh dill,
    or 1½ teaspoons dried dill
½ teaspoon salt
¼ cup pine nuts
3 tablespoons currants
1 cup water
6 tablespoons lemon juice
1½ cups chicken stock (see
    page 26)
2 to 3 lemons, cut into wedges

Blanch fresh grape leaves in hot water for 1 minute; lift out with a slotted spoon and drain. (Or remove grape leaves from jar, scald with hot water, and drain.) Cut off the stems and pat each leaf dry with paper towels. In a large frying pan, sauté the onion in oil until golden. Add the rice, parsley, dill, salt, pine nuts, currants, and water. Cover and simmer 10 minutes, or until liquid is absorbed; let cool. When cool, place 1 teaspoon of the rice mixture in the center of each leaf (shiny surface down), fold like an envelope, and roll up. Do not roll too tightly as rice will expand. Arrange the rolls in layers in a large pot. Pour in the lemon juice and broth. Weight with a baking dish. Cover and simmer 35 minutes, or until rice is tender. Let cool in pan. ☆ Serve chilled, garnished with lemon wedges. Makes 12 servings, about 100 calories each.

☆ Prepare 2 to 3 days in advance to this point and refrigerate.

Fish-Stuffed Tomatoes

¾ pound cold poached snapper, halibut, sole, or turbot
1 tablespoon olive oil
2 tablespoons lemon juice
1 tablespoon white wine vinegar
 Salt
 Freshly ground pepper
4 leaves mint, finely chopped
2 green onions, chopped
3 tablespoons chopped fresh parsley
¼ teaspoon crumbled dried oregano
1 tablespoon pine nuts
4 tomatoes
 Salad greens
1 dozen tiny Mediterranean olives

Flake the fish coarsely into a bowl. Combine the oil, lemon juice, vinegar, salt and pepper to taste, the mint, onions, parsley, oregano, and pine nuts and add to fish, mixing lightly. Core the tomatoes, scoop out the pulp, and reserve it for another use. Spoon the fish salad into the tomato shells and chill until serving time. Serve on greens and garnish with olives. Makes 4 servings, about 150 calories each.

Sorrel Avgolemono Soup

1   bunch green onions, chopped
      (white part only)
1   small bunch sorrel, shredded
      (about ¾ cup leaves)
½ teaspoon butter
3   cups chicken stock (see
      page 26)
2   eggs
1½ tablespoons lemon juice
4   ounces feta cheese
¼ cup coarsely chopped pistachios
2   tablespoons chopped fresh
      chives

Sauté the onions and sorrel in butter until glazed. Add the stock and bring to a boil. Simmer 5 minutes. Purée in a blender or food processor. Beat eggs and lemon juice until blended. Add a little of the hot broth and whisk. Pour this into the pan, add remaining broth, and cook over very low heat, stirring, until thickened. Ladle into bowls and garnish with crumbled cheese, nuts, and chives. Makes 4 servings, about 160 calories each.

Stuffed Apricot Platter

    Citrus or grape leaves
8   apricots
½ pound seedless grapes
    Nasturtium, fuschia, or
      gardenia blossoms

Arrange washed leaves on a platter. Halve and stone the apricots and place them on the leaves. Cut the grapes into very small bunches and nestle a bunch in each apricot half. Garnish with flower blossoms. Makes 4 servings, about 75 calories each.

Supper from Normandy Serves 6

Spinach Platter Salad
Honfleur Fish Stew
Sherried Pears

For an autumn supper in a French mood, begin with a handsome vegetable salad on a bed of spinach, go on to an aromatic fish stew, and finish with hot, wine-glazed pears. For a wine, serve a Muscadet or a Pinot Blanc. The per-person tally for this fish stew supper is about 375 calories.

Spinach Platter Salad

1   **large bunch spinach, stems removed**
¼   **pound mushrooms, sliced**
1   **large red pepper, seeded and diced**
2   **tomatoes, cut in wedges**
1   **small red onion, very finely sliced**
1   **cup alfalfa sprouts**
3   **stalks sweet anise or celery, diced**
   Parmesan Dressing (see below)

Wash spinach thoroughly and pat dry. Tear into bite-sized pieces and place on a large platter or chop plate (about 14 inches in diameter). Arrange the mushrooms, pepper, tomatoes, onion, sprouts, and anise in rows on top. Cover with plastic film and refrigerate until serving time. When ready to serve, pour Parmesan Dressing over all. Makes 6 servings, about 115 calories each.

Parmesan Dressing: Place in a jar ¼ cup olive oil, 2 tablespoons red wine vinegar, 2 tablespoons lemon juice, ¾ teaspoon salt, ½ teaspoon dry mustard, a dash of Worcestershire, and 1 clove garlic, minced. Shake well. Just before serving add ⅓ cup freshly grated Parmesan cheese and shake again.

Honfleur Fish Stew

2 teaspoons butter
1 medium onion, chopped
1 leek, chopped
1 quart clam or chicken stock
   (see page 26)
1 cup dry white wine or vermouth
2 medium baking potatoes, peeled
   and cut into 1-inch pieces

3 carrots, peeled and cut into
   $\frac{1}{2}$-inch pieces
1 bay leaf
$\frac{1}{2}$ teaspoon fennel seed
$1\frac{1}{4}$ pounds boneless red snapper,
   halibut, or rockfish, cut
   into hefty chunks
Salt
Freshly ground pepper

Melt the butter in a large saucepot and sauté the onion and leek, stirring, until soft. Add the chicken stock and wine and bring to a boil. Add potatoes, carrots, bay leaf, and fennel to broth. Bring to a boil, cover, and simmer until vegetables are tender, about 15 to 20 minutes. Add fish to soup, cover, and simmer about 5 minutes or until fish flakes easily with a fork. Season with salt and pepper to taste and ladle into bowls. Makes 6 servings, about 150 calories each.

Sherried Pears

6 medium Bartlett or Anjou pears
1 dozen almonds, finely chopped
2 tablespoons honey
$\frac{1}{2}$ cup dry sherry
$\frac{1}{2}$ teaspoon freshly grated lemon
   peel
$\frac{1}{4}$ teaspoon almond extract

Halve and seed the pears and place in a baking dish. Sprinkle almonds in the pear cavities. Combine the honey, sherry, lemon peel, and almond extract in a saucepan and heat until blended. Spoon this over the pears. Bake covered in a 350° oven for 30 minutes, or just until tender. Serve warm. Makes 6 servings, about 110 calories each.

Mandarin Supper Serves 6

Egg Flower Soup
Oriental Vegetable Relishes with Sea Salt and Soy
Mandarin Rolled Turkey Pancakes
Fruit Basket

With barbecued turkey or chicken on hand, this impromptu Chinese supper can go together instantly. A basket of Oriental vegetables provides an edible centerpiece. Offer jicama, sugar peas, daikon, Chinese cabbage, and other seasonal, crisp vegetables. Serve with sea salt and soy sauce for dipping. Dessert may be a basket of tangerines, kumquats or plums— whatever the market offers. A bottle of Gerwürztraminer goes well here. The calorie count for this Oriental supper is about 350 per person, depending on the vegetables and fruits presented.

Egg Flower Soup

1 quart chicken stock (see
     page 26)
2 teaspoons soy sauce
2 thin slices peeled fresh ginger
     root
¼ cup cooked ham or roast pork,
     in julienne strips
2 green onions, chopped
1 egg

Bring stock to a boil with soy and ginger root. Add the ham and onions. Beat egg until frothy and pour into the hot broth. Remove the pan from heat and swirl with a fork. Makes 6 servings, about 30 calories each.

Mandarin Rolled Turkey Pancakes

6 flour tortillas (about 6 inches in diameter)

3 cups slivered cooked (preferably smoke-barbecued) turkey or chicken

1 tablespoon butter

1 tablespoon soy sauce

1 bunch green onions, chopped

½ cup cilantro sprigs (about 1 bunch)

Hoisin sauce

Place tortillas 2 at a time in a hot, ungreased frying pan. Heat for 30 seconds, turn over, and heat for 30 seconds longer. Then remove from pan and keep warm in a towel (or wrap in aluminum foil and place in a low oven until ready to serve). Sauté turkey in butter with soy sauce just until heated. Assemble hot turkey, onions, cilantro, and hoisin sauce in separate dishes. Let guests fill and roll their own pancakes at the table. Makes 6 servings, about 200 calories each.

Elegant French Supper

Serves 6

Mushroom and Avocado Salad
Steak Tartar with Green Peppercorns
Caramelized Apples Flambé

Here is a swift-to-assemble supper for all seasons. It is a gala menu that can be assembled in minutes, just before a few intimate friends arrive. A raw mushroom salad, enriched with avocado, a green peppercorn-sparked steak tartar, and hot, caramelized apple slices provide a delightful repast. The meal is ready-made for lingering over a fine bottle of Cabernet Sauvignon. The calorie count for this easy supper is 515 per person.

Mushroom and Avocado Salad

Herb Dressing (see below)
¾ pound mushrooms, sliced
1 avocado, peeled and diced
1 cup halved cherry tomatoes
    (about ¼ pound)
    Lettuce
    Chopped fresh parsley

First mix together the Herb Dressing (see below). Place the mushrooms in a bowl, pour on the dressing, and mix lightly. Add avocado and cherry tomatoes and mix again. Spoon out on salad plates lined with lettuce leaves and sprinkle with parsley. Makes 6 servings, about 165 calories each.

Herb Dressing: Mix together 3 tablespoons red wine vinegar, 2 tablespoons dry red wine, 1 tablespoon lemon juice, 2 tablespoons fresh minced chives or green onions, 1 teaspoon chopped fresh tarragon, 1 teaspoon basil, 1 teaspoon oregano, 1 teaspoon Dijon mustard, and 4 tablespoons olive oil.

Steak Tartar with Green Peppercorns

1½ pounds very lean ground top round

3 egg whites

1½ teaspoons salt

¼ teaspoon freshly ground pepper

2 teaspoons Worcestershire

2 teaspoons Dijon mustard

4 teaspoons red wine vinegar

2 teaspoons green peppercorns, rinsed and chopped

¼ cup finely chopped shallots or green onions

2 tablespoons chopped fresh parsley

2 cloves garlic, finely chopped

Watercress or butter lettuce

1 cup halved cherry tomatoes

Place in a mixing bowl the ground meat, egg whites, salt, pepper, Worcestershire, mustard, vinegar, chopped peppercorns, shallots, parsley, and garlic and mix until blended. Shape into 6 patties and arrange on individual plates. Ring with watercress sprigs or small lettuce leaves and halved tomatoes. Makes 6 servings, about 225 calories each.

Caramelized Apples Flambé

1 tablespoon butter

3 tablespoons sugar

6 Golden Delicious or cooking apples, peeled and thinly sliced

3 tablespoons Calvados, cognac, or brandy

Melt the butter and sugar together in a large frying pan. Add the apple slices and sauté until glazed and golden brown. Heat the Calvados and ignite a spoonful. Return this to pan so the remainder ignites, and spoon it, flaming, over the apples. Makes 6 servings, about 125 calories each.

Supper from Genoa $\quad$ Serves 6

Chicken Soup with Pesto
Sweet Pepper and Tomato Salad
Pineapple with Almond Crunch

A rich chicken soup laced with vegetables and sprinkled with shredded Gruyère and pesto sauce offers a rewarding entrée for a late supper or luncheon. A harvest salad with sweet red peppers makes a piquant beginning. For dessert, serve fresh pineapple topped with a caramelized crunch of almonds. Offer a Chenin Blanc with the meal. The calorie count for this Italian supper is about 500 per person.

Chicken Soup with Pesto

1½ quarts chicken stock, or 1½ quarts water and 6 chicken bouillon cubes
1 onion, quartered
¼ cup celery leaves
1 broiler-fryer (3½ pounds)
½ teaspoon salt
⅛ teaspoon freshly ground pepper

4 carrots, peeled and sliced
2 leeks, chopped
1 stalk celery, chopped
2 medium turnips, peeled and diced
Pesto Sauce (see page 122)
1 cup freshly grated Gruyère or jarlsberg cheese

In a large soup kettle bring the stock to a boil. Add the onion, celery leaves, and whole chicken. Season with the salt and pepper, cover, and simmer 1 hour, or until chicken is tender. Remove from pot and let cool slightly. Remove the skin and bones and cut the chicken meat into large strips. Strain the stock and skim the fat. ☆ Bring the stock to a boil and add the carrots, leeks, celery, and turnips. Cover and simmer 15 minutes, or until vegetables are crisp tender. Add chicken strips and heat thoroughly. Ladle into soup bowls and pass bowls of Pesto Sauce and cheese separately. Makes 6 servings, about 310 calories each.

☆ Prepare in advance to this point and refrigerate.

Sweet Pepper and Tomato Salad

3 tablespoons olive oil
2 tablespoons red wine vinegar
½ teaspoon salt
⅛ teaspoon freshly ground pepper
1 tablespoon chopped fresh basil,
   or ¾ teaspoon dried basil
1 red pepper, seeded and
   chopped

1 green pepper, seeded and
   chopped
1 sweet red onion, chopped
⅓ cup chopped fresh parsley
   Greens
4 large tomatoes, peeled and
   sliced

Mix together in a bowl the oil, vinegar, salt, pepper, and basil. Add the peppers, onion, and parsley and chill 1 hour. Place greens on a platter and cover with sliced tomatoes. Spoon on the marinated vegetables and the dressing. Makes 6 servings, about 90 calories each.

Pineapple with Almond Crunch

2 teaspoons butter
1 tablespoon sugar
6 tablespoons slivered almonds or
   chopped pistachios or pecans

1 medium pineapple
2 tablespoons rum

Place the butter and sugar in a small frying pan and cook at medium heat until butter melts. Add the nuts and stir to coat them evenly. Cook just until lightly browned, then turn onto a buttered sheet of foil and let cool. Break up to separate nuts. ☆ Halve pineapple lengthwise, core, and scoop out the fruit with a grapefruit knife. Cut into bite-sized pieces. Place fruit in a bowl and spoon rum on top. Let chill for several hours. To serve, spoon into dessert bowls and sprinkle with nut crunch. Makes 6 servings, about 100 calories each.

☆ Prepare several days in advance to this point. Store in an airtight container.

Clam Diggers' Sundown Supper

Serves 6

Hot Clams in Garlic Butter
Toasted Walnut and Gruyère Salad
Wine-Steeped Fruit Bowl

If you are fortunate enough to dig your own clams, this is a superb way to savor the fruits of your labor, but any small, store-bought clams, such as rock or butter clams, will work well. A buttery wine sauce permeates the meat during broiling. A cheese and walnut salad provides a hearty side dish. For dessert, the season's fruits show off in a wine-steeped compote. A Pinot Blanc or a very dry chilled sherry would complement the seafood. The total count for this light continental supper is 420 calories per person.

Hot Clams in Garlic Butter

5 dozen fresh clams
½ cup dry white wine
2 tablespoons butter
1 tablespoon minced fresh
     parsley
2 cloves garlic, minced
2 shallots or green onions, finely
     chopped
4 tablespoons fine dry bread
     crumbs
4 tablespoons freshly grated
     Parmesan or Romano cheese

Scrub clams thoroughly. Place in a pot with the wine and steam until the shells open. Break off and discard the empty half shells. Arrange the filled half shells on a shallow baking pan. Boil down the broth until reduced to ½ cup. Add butter, parsley, garlic, and shallots and heat to blend. Spoon this over the clams on the shells and sprinkle with a mixture of crumbs and cheese. Place under the broiler and broil until lightly browned and hot, about 2 minutes. Serve about 10 clams on the half shell to each person. Makes 6 servings, about 135 calories each.

Toasted Walnut and Gruyère Salad

¼ cup safflower oil
2 tablespoons red wine vinegar
1 tablespoon Dijon mustard
1 green onion, minced
½ teaspoon salt
⅛ teaspoon freshly ground pepper
2 heads butter lettuce

1 tablespoon finely chopped fresh chives and parsley, mixed together
1 cup freshly grated Gruyère or jarlsberg cheese (4 ounces)
½ cup toasted walnut halves
2 tomatoes, cut into wedges, or 1 cup halved cherry tomatoes

For dressing, blend together the oil, vinegar, mustard, onion, and salt and pepper. Chill. Place walnuts in a shallow pan and roast in a 325° oven for 10 to 15 minutes, or until lightly toasted. Tear washed, crisped lettuce into bite-sized pieces and place in a salad bowl. Add the chives and parsley. Pour in the dressing and mix lightly. Spoon onto individual salad plates and sprinkle with cheese and walnut halves. Ring the salads with tomatoes. Makes 6 servings, about 185 calories each.

Wine-Steeped Fruit Bowl

1 cup fruity white wine, such as Johannisberg Riesling or Chenin Blanc
2 tablespoons orange liqueur
1 tablespoon sugar

1 cup watermelon balls
1 cup honeydew melon balls
1 cup cantaloupe balls
1½ cups strawberries
Mint sprigs

Mix together the wine, liqueur, and sugar. Make one layer each of the watermelon, honeydew, cantaloupe, and berries in a serving bowl. Pour in the wine mixture, cover, and chill. Spoon into bowls and garnish with mint. Makes 6 servings, about 85 calories each.

$\mathcal{A}$ Scandinavian Supper Serves 6

Eggs and Caviar
Swedish Liver Loaf
Borscht
Apple Snow

This colorful supper can be set out with ease at the last minute. It makes an excellent midday meal, as well. The liver loaf, egg spread, and soup may all be done in advance. The fresh apple snow is an on-the-spot item. Pass a Gamay or Grignolino wine for accompaniment. The calorie count for this winter luncheon or supper is about 405 per person.

Eggs and Caviar

6   hard-cooked eggs
2   tablespoons yogurt
2   tablespoons sour cream
2   green onions, finely chopped
½   teaspoon Dijon mustard
½   teaspoon salt
¼   teaspoon freshly ground pepper
     or 1 teaspoon green
     peppercorns, finely chopped
4   ounces black caviar
1   bunch green onions, finely
     chopped

Shred the eggs with a food processor or grate them manually. Mix in the yogurt, sour cream, onions, mustard, and salt and pepper. Mound in a bowl and chill. Spoon caviar into a bowl and chill. At serving time offer bowls of egg, caviar, and more chopped green onions to spread on flat-bread or rye crisps. If desired, the Swedish Liver Loaf can be served with the egg spread. Makes 6 servings, allowing 2 or 3 topped crackers per person, about 150 calories per serving.

Swedish Liver Loaf

1   small onion, chopped
1½ pounds cooked calf's liver,
      cubed
⅓   pound cooked lean pork
      . sausage
1   cup beef or chicken stock (see
      page 38 or page 26)
3   tablespoons nonfat dry milk
3   eggs
1½ teaspoons salt
1   teaspoon Worcestershire
¼   teaspoon cinnamon
¼   teaspoon allspice
¼   teaspoon nutmeg
¼   teaspoon cloves
¼   teaspoon freshly ground pepper
      Watercress

Sauté the onion in a dry frying pan for 5 minutes, stirring occasionally. In a food processor or blender, purée the liver, sausage, and onion. Turn into a bowl and mix in the beef stock, powdered milk, eggs, salt, Worcestershire, cinnamon, allspice, nutmeg, cloves, and pepper. Spoon into a buttered 9 by 5-inch loaf pan and cover with foil. Place in a pan containing 1 inch of hot water and bake in a 350° oven for 1 hour; remove the foil and bake ½ hour longer. Cool, then chill. ☆ To serve, turn onto a platter and garnish with watercress. Makes 12 servings, about 110 calories each.

☆ Prepare up to 3 days in advance to this point and refrigerate.

Borscht

1 bunch (5 medium) peeled beets, with greens	1 teaspoon salt
	¼ teaspoon freshly ground pepper
2 carrots, peeled	2 tablespoons cornstarch
1 large onion	2 tablespoons cold water
1 tablespoon butter	Plain yogurt or sour
2 quarts beef stock (see page 38)	half-and-half
¼ cup red wine vinegar	Lemon slices
1 teaspoon brown sugar	

Trim the greens from the beets and finely chop. Sprinkle the greens with salt and let them stand 5 minutes, then rinse thoroughly. Shred the peeled beets, carrots, and onion and sauté them in the butter until glazed, using a large soup kettle. Pour in the beef stock and add the vinegar, sugar, salt, and pepper. Cover and simmer 30 minutes, or until vegetables are very tender. Add the greens to the soup and simmer 5 minutes longer. ☆ Ladle into bowls and garnish with yogurt and lemon slices. Makes 6 servings, about 55 calories each.

☆ Prepare in advance to this point and refrigerate.

Apple Snow

1½ tablespoons orange blossom
      honey
¼ cup lemon juice
6 tart, crisp apples, peeled and
      cored
2 ice cubes
   Ground cinnamon or mint sprigs

In a bowl, stir together the honey and lemon juice until honey dissolves. Grate the apples and mix them in. Crush the ice and mix with the apple. Dust with cinnamon or garnish with a sprig of mint and serve at once. Makes 6 servings, about 90 calories each.

After~Theatre Supper
Serves 8

Buttercup Curried Soup
Spicy Orange Veal Patties
Wheat Germ Rounds
Relish Basket
Herb Dip
Grape Parfait

This versatile menu suits many occasions and seasons—a spring after-theatre supper, a summer sailing picnic, or a harvest wine tasting. The golden curry soup is excellent hot or cold, as are the spicy meat patties served on whole-grain bread rounds. Arrange a fresh relish tray for dipping in the herb sauce. For dessert, grapes are dressed in a brown sugar-yogurt mixture that slowly turns to syrup during chilling. A Gamay Rosé or Gewürztraminer wine would go nicely with the meal. Allow 585 calories per person.

Buttercup Curried Soup

1 large tart apple, peeled and
    diced
1 large onion, minced
1 teaspoon butter
1 teaspoon curry powder
4 cups chicken stock (see
    page 26)
½ teaspoon salt
¼ teaspoon freshly ground pepper
¼ cup dry sherry
2 tablespoons sour cream
¼ cup plain yogurt
2 tablespoons chopped fresh
    chives or parsley

Using a large saucepot, sauté the apple and onion in butter with the curry powder until glazed. Add the stock and simmer 25 minutes. Season with the salt and pepper. Let cool slightly, then purée in a blender. Reheat and ladle into bowls. Mix the sour cream and yogurt together and spoon a little over each serving. Sprinkle with chives. Makes 8 servings, about 50 calories each.

Spicy Orange Veal Patties

2 pounds lean ground veal
½ pound lean ground pork
1 teaspoon cinnamon
1 teaspoon allspice
2 teaspoons salt
½ teaspoon freshly ground pepper
3 cloves garlic, minced
¼ cup finely chopped fresh parsley

1 tablespoon freshly grated orange peel
1 green onion or shallot, chopped
⅓ cup dry white wine
⅓ cup rich chicken stock (see page 26)
2 eggs
2 teaspoons butter

Mix together in a bowl the meats, cinnamon, allspice, salt, pepper, garlic, parsley, orange peel, onion, wine, stock, and eggs. Melt 1 teaspoon of the butter in a large frying pan and drop in the meat mixture by tablespoonfuls, forming small oval patties. Cook about half the total mixture at once. Brown patties on both sides. Remove from the pan and keep them warm. Repeat, cooking the remaining meat patties in the last teaspoon butter. ☆ Makes 10 servings, about 250 calories each.

☆ Prepare in advance to this point and refrigerate. Reheat to serve.

Wheat Germ Rounds

3 cups unbleached flour (approximately)
3 cups whole wheat flour
⅓ cup wheat germ
2 teaspoons salt

2 packages active dry yeast
2½ cups very warm water (125°)
¼ cup honey
3 tablespoons soft butter

Place in a large mixing bowl 1 cup of the unbleached flour, 1 cup of the whole wheat flour, and the wheat germ. Add the salt and yeast and stir to blend. Pour in the water and beat until smooth. Mix in the honey and butter. Add the remaining whole wheat flour and beat for 5 minutes. Gradually add the remaining unbleached flour, adding just enough to make a stiff dough. Turn onto a floured board and knead for 5 to 10 minutes. Place in a greased bowl, butter the top, cover with a towel, and let rise in a warm place until doubled in size, about 1½ hours. Punch down, divide dough in quarters, and shape them into balls. Place the balls in 4 greased 1-pound coffee cans. Cover and let rise until doubled in size, about 45 minutes. Bake in a 375° oven for 30 minutes, or until loaves sound hollow when thumped. Let cool 5 minutes, then remove from cans. ☆ Each loaf makes 6 to 8 servings, about 50 calories per slice.

☆ Prepare in advance to this point and freeze, wrapped, when loaves have cooled slightly.

Herb Dip

⅔ cup plain yogurt
⅓ cup sour cream
1 clove garlic, minced
2 tablespoons minced fresh parsley
2 tablespoons chopped fresh chives
1 shallot, chopped
2 teaspoons chopped fresh tarragon or basil

Mix together all ingredients. Spoon into a serving bowl, cover, and chill. Serve with fresh vegetables. Makes 8 servings, about 100 calories each.

Grape Parfait

8 cups seedless grapes
8 tablespoons sour cream
8 tablespoons plain yogurt
4 tablespoons brown sugar

Wash and stem the grapes and pat dry. Mix together the sour cream and yogurt. Alternate layers of grapes and sour cream in parfait glasses, sprinkling some sugar on each sour cream layer. Each glass should have two layers of each. End with sour cream and a final dash of sugar. Chill briefly before serving. Makes 8 servings, about 135 calories each.

Aperitifs and Other Beverages

Wine aperitifs are very much in vogue today because they offer a fine way to prelude a meal—they have fewer calories and less impact than liquor. They are also easily extended with mineral water, soda, or fruit juice for taller, longer-lasting drinks. Here is a choice of refreshers.

Royals

Spoon 1½ tablespoons rasberry juice or 2 teaspoons Framboise liqueur into each chilled champagne glass and pour in Champagne to fill.

Strawberry Spritzers

1 bottle (about 26 ounces) Gewürztraminer or Chenin Blanc
¾ cup strawberry wine or strawberry juice
1 lemon, thinly sliced
1 8-ounce bottle club soda or mineral water
8 large strawberries

Mix together in a pitcher the wine, strawberry wine, and lemon slices; chill. Just before serving add the soda. Pour into ice-filled glasses and float a whole berry in each. Makes 8 servings, about 105 calories each.

Kir

1 bottle (about 26 ounces) dry white wine, such as Pinot Blanc, Mountain White Chablis, or Pouilly-Fuissé
¼ cup imported crème de cassis liqueur*

Chill wine thoroughly and combine with the crème de cassis in a pitcher. Serve in wine glasses. Makes 8 servings, about 100 calories each.

* Different brands of this liqueur vary in strength, so adjust proportions accordingly.

Cassis Chablis

3½ ounces Chablis or dry vermouth
1 tablespoon crème de cassis
   liqueur
½ cup mineral water or club soda
   Strip of lemon peel

Place ice in a pilsner or other tall glass. Pour in Chablis and add liqueur, stirring to blend. Pour in the mineral water and garnish with lemon peel. Makes 1 serving, about 115 calories.

Burgundy Spritzer

3½ ounces Burgundy
   Few drops lime juice
½ cup club soda or mineral water
   Slice of lime

Pour the wine, lime juice, and soda water in a tall glass containing 2 ice cubes. Stir to blend and garnish with a slice of lime. Makes 1 serving, about 85 calories.

Mimosas

3¼ cups orange juice
1 bottle (about 26 ounces)
   Champagne

Combine chilled orange juice and Champagne in a pitcher. Pour into well-chilled champagne glasses and serve at once. Makes 10 servings, about 120 calories each.

Orange Refresher

2 tablespoons undiluted orange
   juice concentrate
½ cup mineral water
   Twist of lemon

Spoon concentrate into a glass and pour in mineral water, stirring to blend. Garnish with lemon twist. Makes 1 serving, about 60 calories.

Burgundy Tonic

3½ ounces Burgundy
   Sugar-free tonic water
   Wedge of lime

Place 2 ice cubes in a tall glass; pour in wine and ⅓ to ½ cup tonic. Squeeze lime over drink and drop wedge into glass. Makes 1 serving, about 85 calories.

Sangria

1 bottle (about 26 ounces) dry
   red wine (Burgundy or
   Zinfandel)
2 cups orange juice

1 lemon, very thinly sliced
1 orange, very thinly sliced and
   cut in half moons*
1 8-ounce bottle club soda

Chill all beverages thoroughly. In a pitcher, combine the wine, orange juice, and sliced fruit and chill 20 minutes. Pour in the soda. Serve in ice-filled glasses with a slice of citrus floating in each. Makes 10 servings, about 100 calories each.

* For even more Spanish flavor, add slices of apples, pears, and peaches and let all the fruit steep overnight in the wine. Add a cinnamon stick a few minutes before serving.

Mineral Water Tasting

The tremendous variety of mineral waters are a fine excuse for a tasting, sans calories. Present three or more well-chilled waters, with a separate glass for each. The flavors are amazingly varied.

Citrus Water

For a most refreshing drink, also sans calories, float a wafer-thin slice of lemon or lime in a wide-bowled glass filled with ice cubes or crushed ice and water. Old-fashioned sundae glasses or large-bowled wine glasses work very well.

The Calorie Counter

Food	Weight in Grams	Approximate Measure	Calories
Almonds, shelled	142	1 cup	850
Apple, raw	150	1 med.	70
Apricots, raw	114	3 apricots	55
dried	150	1 cup (40 halves)	390
Artichokes, cooked	100	1 lg. bud (base and soft end of leaves)	51
Jerusalem, raw	100	4 sm., 1½-inch dia.	70
Asparagus, fresh	60	4 spears	10
pieces	145	1 cup	30
Avocados, whole raw fruit	284	California, 3⅛-in. dia.	370
	454	Florida, 3⅝-in. dia.	390
Bacon, broiled or fried	15	2 slices	90
Bamboo shoots	100	¾ cup	25
Banana, raw	150	1 med.	85
Beans, green, fresh cooked	125	1 cup	30
lima, fresh cooked	160	1 cup	180
Bean sprouts, mung	77	1¾ cup	23
Beef			
braised or pot-roasted, lean and fat	112	4 oz.	330
hamburger, lean, broiled	112	4 oz.	250
hamburger, regular, broiled	112	4 oz.	330
roast, rib	112	4 oz.	500
rump or heel round	112	4 oz.	220
steak, round	112	4 oz.	220
sirloin	112	4 oz.	440
Beets, fresh cooked	100	2 whole	30

Food	Weight in Grams	Approximate Measure	Calories
Beverages			
alcoholic			
beer	360	12 fl. oz.	150
Gin, rum, vodka,			
whiskey, 90-proof	42	1½ oz.	110
Wines, dessert	103	3½ fl. oz.	140
Wines, table	102	3½ fl. oz.	85
Carbonated water	366	12 fl. oz.	115
Coffee and tea	—	—	0
Cola type	369	12 fl. oz.	145
Ginger ale	366	12 fl. oz.	115
Liqueurs, brandy or			
Cognac	30	1 brandy glass	73
creme de menthe	20	1 cordial glass	67
Curacao	20	1 cordial glass	54
Root beer	370	12 fl. oz.	150
Blueberries	140	1 cup	85
Bouillon cubes	4	1 cube, about ½ in.	5
Brazil nuts, shelled	15	4 average	97
Bread, white enriched	23	1 slice	60
whole wheat	23	1 slice	55
French or Italian	454	1 lb. loaf	1315
Broccoli	155	1 cup, cooked	40
Brussels sprouts	155	7 to 8 sprouts	55
Butter	14	1 tablespoon	100
Buttermilk, made from			
skim milk	245	1 cup	90
Cabbage, shredded, raw	100	1 cup	25
Chinese	100	1 cup	15

Food	Weight in Grams	Approximate Measure	Calories
Cakes, angel	53	¹⁄₁₂ of 10-in. cake	135
pound	30	½-in. slice (3 by 3 in.)	140
sponge	66	¹⁄₁₂ of 10-in. cake	195
Candy: caramel or fudge	28	1 oz.	115
peanut brittle	25	1 piece	110
Cantaloupe, raw	385	½ of 5-in. melon	60
Carrots	50	1 carrot	20
Cashew nuts	135	1 cup	760
Cauliflower, raw	100	1 cup	25
Celery	40	1 stalk	5
Chard, leaves and stalks	100	½ cup cooked	21
Cheese—Swiss, Cheddar,			
Roquefort, or Blue	28	1 oz.	105
Camembert	28	1 oz.	84
Cottage cheese	225	1 cup	240
Cream cheese	15	1 tablespoon	55
Parmesan	28	1 oz.	110
Ricotta	225	1 cup	400
Cherries, raw sweet	130	1 cup	80
Chicken, fresh, broiled	85	3 oz.	115
Chicory or endive, curly	50	15 to 20 inner leaves	10
Chili sauce	17	1 tablespoon	20
Chocolate, bitter or baking	28	1 oz.	145
semisweet, small pieces	170	1 cup	860
Clams, raw	85	3 oz.	65
canned, solids and liquid	85	3 oz.	45
Coconut, fresh	97	1 cup, shredded	335
dried, sweetened	62	1 cup, shredded	340
Cookies, plain and assorted	25	1 cookie, 3-in. dia.	120
Corn	140	1 ear, 5 in. long	70
Cornstarch	8	1 tablespoon	29
Crabmeat, canned	85	3 oz.	85
Crackers, graham	28	4 squares	110
saltines	11	4 squares	50

Food	Weight in Grams	Approximate Measure	Calories
Cream, half-and-half	15	1 tablespoon	20
heavy or whipping	15	1 tablespoon	50
sour	15	1 tablespoon	50
sour half-and-half	15	1 tablespoon	30
Cucumber	207	12 in. by 7 in.	30
Dandelion greens, cooked	90	½ cup	40
Dates	178	1 cup	490
Eggplant	100	2 slices or ½ cup	24
Eggs	50	1 med.	80
egg white	33	1 white	15
egg yolk	17	1 yolk	60
Fats, cooking, vegetable	12.5	1 tablespoon	110
Figs, dried	21	1 fig	60
Filberts	15	10 to 12 nuts	95
Flour, enriched	100	⅞ cup	350
whole wheat	100	¾ cup	333
Gelatin, plain dry powder	7	1 envelope	25
Gooseberries, raw	100	⅔ cup	39
Grapefuit, raw, white	241	½ grapefruit, 3¾-in. dia.	45
raw, pink	241	½ grapefruit, 3¾-in. dia.	50
juice, fresh	246	1 cup	45
Grape juice, canned or bottled	246	1 cup	165
Grapes, raw Concord, Niagara	153	1 cup	65
Muscat, Thompson, Tokay	160	1 cup	95
Honey	21	1 tablespoon	65
Ice cream, regular (10% fat)	133	1 cup	255
rich (approx. 16% fat)	148	1 cup	330
Ice milk, hardened	131	1 cup	200
soft-serve	175	1 cup	265
Jams, preserves, jellies	20	1 tablespoon	55
Lamb, chop, broiled	137	1 chop, 4¼-in. dia.	400
leg, roasted, lean and fat	112	4 oz.	305
lean only	64	2.3 oz.	130

Food	Weight in Grams	Approximate Measure	Calories
Leeks	100	3 or 4, 5 in. long	40
Lemon	106	1 med.	20
juice (or lime juice), fresh	15	1 tablespoon	5
Lentils	95	½ cup, cooked	100
Lettuce, iceberg	464	1 head, 4¼-in. dia.	60
leaves	50	2 lg. leaves	10
Liver, beef, raw	100	2 slices	136
calf, raw	100	2 slices	141
chicken, raw	100	2 large	140
Lobster, canned	85	½ cup	75
Macadamia nuts	15	8 to 12	108
Mangos	100	1 sm.	60
Margarine, regular	14	1 tablespoon	100
stick (4 sticks to pound)	113	½ cup	815
whipped (6 sticks per pound) stick	76	½ cup	545
Milk, whole	244	1 cup	160
dry, nonfat, instant	70	1 cup	250
low fat, 2%	246	1 cup	145
nonfat, skim	245	1 cup	90
Mushrooms, fresh	100	10 sm. or 4 lg.	16
Nectarines	100	2 med.	60
Oils, salad or cooking, corn, olive, peanut, safflower, or soybean	14	1 tablespoon	125
Olives, green	16	4 med. or 3 extra lg.	15
ripe	10	3 sm. or 2 lg.	15
Onions, raw, yellow	110	1 onion, 2½-in. dia.	40
young green, without tops	50	6 onions	20
Orange, navel	180	1 med.	65
juice, fresh	248	1 cup	110
frozen reconstituted	249	1 cup	120
Oysters, raw	240	1 cup	160
Papayas	182	1 cup, ½-in. cubes	70
Parsley, raw chopped	4	1 tablespoon	trace
Parsnips, cooked	155	1 cup	100

Food	Weight in Grams	Approximate Measure	Calories
Passion fruit	100	½ cup	71
Peaches	114	1 peach, 2-in. dia.	35
Peanut butter	16	1 tablespoon	95
Peanuts, roasted, salted, halves	144	1 cup	840
Pears, raw	182	1 med. pear	100
Peas, edible pod	100	29 to 33 pods	31
green, fresh cooked	160	1 cup	115
Peppers, green, raw	62	1 med.	15
Persimmons	100	1 med.	78
Pickles, dill	135	1 pickle, 4 in. long	15
sweet	20	1 pickle, 2¾ in. long	30
Pie, apple or cherry	135	⅐ of 9-in. pie	350
pecan	118	⅐ of 9-in. pie	490
Pimientos	35	canned, medium	9
Pineapple, raw	140	1 cup, diced	75
canned, syrup pack	260	1 cup, crushed	195
juice, canned	249	1 cup	135
sliced	122	1 lg. slice	135
Pine nuts (pignolias)	15	¼ cup, scant	85
Pistachio nuts	15	30 nuts	88
Pizza, cheese	75	5½-in. sector	185
Plums, raw	60	1 plum	25
Pork, chop	98	1 chop, 3.5 oz.	260
ham, cured	112	4 oz.	325
roast, lean and fat	112	4 oz.	410
Potatoes, baked	99	1 med.	90
Prunes, dried	25	3 med.	67
juice, canned or bottled	256	1 cup	200
Pumpkin, canned	228	1 cup	75
Radishes	40	4 sm.	5
Raisins, seedless	160	1 cup	460
Raspberries, raw	123	1 cup	70
frozen, 10-oz. carton	284	1 carton	275

Food	Weight in Grams	Approximate Measure	Calories
Rhubarb, cooked, sugar added	272	1 cup	385
Rice, white, cooked	168	1 cup	185
Salad dressings, french	16	1 tablespoon	65
Mayonnaise	14	1 tablespoon	100
Salmon, fresh	95	4 oz.	291
smoked	50	2 to 3 slices	89
Sauerkraut, canned	235	1 cup	45
Sausage, bologna	26	2 slices	80
braunschweiger	20	2 slices	80
frankfurter	51	1 frankfurter	155
salami, dry	28	1 oz.	130
Scallops	100	2 or 3	78
Sherbert, orange	193	1 cup	260
Shrimp	112	4 oz.	135
Sole, turbot, red snapper	100	3-by-3-by-⅞-in. piece	156
Soybeans, dried, whole	100	½ cup, dry	331
curd	100	1 cake, 2½ by 2½ by 1 in.	71
Spinach, cooked	180	1 cup	40
Squash, cooked summer	210	1 cup	30
winter	205	1 cup	130
Strawberries, raw	149	1 cup	55
Sugar, brown	14	1 tablespoon	50
white, granulated	12	1 tablespoon	45
white, powdered	8	1 tablespoon	30
Sweet potatoes, baked	110	1 med.	155
Tangerine	114	1 med.	40
Tomato, raw	200	1 med.	40
juice	243	1 cup	45
ketchup	15	1 tablespoon	15
Tuna, canned in oil, drained	85	4 oz.	230
Turkey, roasted	100	3 slices	200
Turnips	155	1 cup	35

Food	Weight in Grams	Approximate Measure	Calories
Veal, cutlet	112	4 oz.	225
roast, lean and fat	112	4 oz.	305
Vinegar	15	1 tablespoon	trace
Walnuts, black or English			
chopped	126	1 cup	790
Water chestnuts	25	4 chestnuts	17
Watercress	10	10 sprigs	2
Watermelon, raw	925	1 wedge, 4 by 8 in.	115
Yogurt, made from partially			
skimmed milk	245	1 cup	125
made from whole milk	245	1 cup	150 to 160

[1]From *Nutritive Value of Foods,* Home and Garden Bull. No. 72 revised (Washington, D.C.: U.S. Dept. Agr., 1971) and certain items from "Food Values of Portions Commonly Used," Bowes and Church, 9th ed. (Philadelphia: Lippincott).

Daily Energy Allowances

	Years (up to)	Weight		Height		Energy in Calories
Infants	.0 to .5	6 kg.	14 lb.	60 cm.	24 in.	kg × 117
	.5 to 1	9	20	71	28	kg × 108
Children	1 to 3	13	28	86	34	1300
	4 to 6	20	44	110	44	1800
	7 to 10	30	66	135	54	2400
Males	11 to 14	44	97	158	63	2800
	15 to 18	61	134	172	69	3000
	19 to 22	67	147	172	69	3000
	23 to 50	70	154	172	69	2700
	51 +	70	154	172	69	2400
Females	11 to 14	44	97	155	62	2400
	15 to 18	54	119	162	65	2100
	19 to 22	58	128	162	65	2100
	23 to 50	58	128	162	65	2000
	51 +	58	128	162	65	1800
Pregnant						+ 300
Lactating						+ 500

From *Recommended Daily Dietary Allowances, Eighth Edition*, Natl. Acad. Sci.-Natl. Research Council Publ. No. 2216 (Washington, D.C.: Natl. Research Council, 1974).

Index